ROAD TO THE CHAMPIONSHIP
SUPER COLTS!

The Indianapolis Star's writers and photographers
chronicle the Colts' run to the Super Bowl

THE INDIANAPOLIS STAR
INDYSTAR★.COM

It was a wild season of ups and downs for The Indianapolis Colts. Certainly, the "ups" dominated. The first nine games without a loss — for the second year in a row. A perfect record at home in the RCA Dome, including the heart-stopping AFC Championship win against the New England Patriots. Then came the season finale — a convincing Super Bowl victory over the Chicago Bears in rainy Miami. Through it all, the writers and photographers for The Indianapolis Star and IndyStar.com were there. Our veteran journalists chronicled it all for the hundreds of thousands of Hoosier readers of The Star — and for Colts' fans worldwide on IndyStar.com.

We decided that a season like this warrants this book highlighting the work of The Star's sports and photo staffs. The fact that you are reading this means you agree. Contributors are profiled on Page 4.

Thanks to the Colts for providing us with five, action-packed months of entertainment, drama and euphoria.

We are pleased to share The Star's fabulous photography and our writers' insights on this wonderful football story.

— **Barbara Henry**
President and Publisher, The Indianapolis Star

Published by Pediment Publishing, a division of The Pediment Group, Inc. www.pediment.com Printed in Canada.

CONTENTS

THE WRITERS & PHOTOGRAPHERS

MIKE CHAPPELL

Sportswriter Mike Chappell came to The Star the same year the Colts arrived from Baltimore in 1984 and has covered the team ever since. He grew up in just south of Indianapolis, "on the poor side of U.S. 40," earned a journalism degree at Ball State University and was sports editor at the Anderson (Ind.) Bulletin before coming to The Star. Mike is member of the Pro Football Hall of Fame selection committee.

MATT DETRICH

Since joining The Star's photography team in 1999, Matt Detrich has won several first-place awards for photojournalism, including Indiana News Photographer of the Year (2001 and 2005), Region 4 Photojournalist of the Year (2001), and National Press Photographers Association's best of photojournalism contest. A 1994 graduate of Ohio University, Matt served five internships and worked at The Medina (Ohio) County Gazette and the Akron Beacon Journal. He and his wife, Tammy, have two daughters, Lauren and Lindsay.

BOB KRAVITZ

A 1982 Indiana University graduate, Bob Kravitz grew up near Chicago and was a sports columnist at The Plain Dealer in Cleveland and The Rocky Mountain News in Denver before coming to The Star in 2000. He writes four columns a week. Bob is married, has two teenaged daughters and two cats. In his spare time, he attempts to play something resembling golf.

MATT KRYGER

A South Dakota native photographer Matt Kryger earned his journalism degree at South Dakota State in 1994 (with a minor in religion) and first worked at The Star as an intern that summer. He returned in 1998 and has covered the Colts ever since. The Star's Photographer of the Year in 2000 (and runner-up in 1999), Matt is a single father of two lovely girls, Madison and McKenna, who are the love of his life.

PHIL RICHARDS

Phil Richards has been a member of The Star's sportswriting team since 1984 and has covered the Colts since 1999. A native of Northern Michigan, Phil is a University of Notre Dame honors graduate and a Vietnam veteran. He wrote for the South Bend Tribune before coming to The Star and has received several first place awards for sportswriting. Phil and his wife, Joan, have two sons, Phil and Denton, and a daughter, Jenna.

SAM RICHE

Sam Riche started taking photographs as a sophomore in high school in Brown County, Indiana, and went on to earn his journalism degree at Indiana University. Before joining The Star's staff in 2004, he worked as a photographer for the Lexington (Ky.) Herald-Leader, The Times of Northwest Indiana and The Herald (Rockhill, S.C.), and as a page designer for The Times of Northwest Indiana and The Herald-Leader. He and his wife, Epha, have two sons, Will and Ben.

ROBERT SCHEER

Kansas native Robert Scheer grew up in California, where he graduated from Humboldt State University in 1994. A biology major, he also played jazz trumpet and sax and edited a creative writing journal. Robert worked as a photographer for several California newspapers before coming to The Star in 1998. He has won several photojournalism awards and works with Indiana's Latino community. An avid cyclist, Robert has studied and traveled in Mexico.

PHILLIP B. WILSON

Phillip B. Wilson has been writing for The Star since 1995 and has a decade of NFL experience — six years on the Colts for The Star and four years covering Cleveland Browns home games for USA Today and Gannett News Service. He is the proud father of two children, Morgan and Brandon. Phil E. celebrated his 42nd birthday at Super Bowl XLI media day in Miami. And yes, he is a fake blond.

OTHER CONTRIBUTORS

Editors: Michael Jesse and Jim Lefko
Photo Editors: Mike Fender, Matt Kryger, Sam Riche, Robert Scheer and Scott Goldman
Designers: Brad Fenison and Scott Goldman
Copy Editor: Geoff Ooley

Special thanks to Dawn Mitchell, Sylvia Halladay, Cathy Knapp, Brian Priester, James Burnes, Phil Mahoney and Phyllis Mahoney for their assistance with this book. Thanks also to the many staffers at The Star who covered the Indianapolis Colts this year — and to the Colts themselves for giving us all such an exciting season.

Colts bring Super Bowl championship to Indy

BOB KRAVITZ

They belong to Indianapolis, first and foremost, a hometown's proud and worthy world champion. But now, these Super Colts, dominant 29-17 winners over the Chicago Bears in Super Bowl XLI, belong, too, to history.

In the end, with a warm, cleansing rain continuing to fall at Dolphin Stadium, Tony Dungy became the first black coach to raise the Lombardi Trophy in victory. As it was once written of Joe Louis, he is a credit to his race — the human race.

He not only shattered a racial barrier, but he proved that yes, hallelujah yes, good guys can still finish first, even in a sport as tough and brutal as professional football.

Even as Dungy stood at the very height of his profession, there was his son Eric joining his father for a snapshot as they stood together on a media podium. Eric gestured with his hand, noting the disparity in stature.

"Still taller than him," Eric said of his father.

On this day, though, nobody stood taller than Dungy, who, like his team, traveled a long and often painful road to this monumental day.

As Dungy spoke, Peyton Manning was across the way addressing the media. And no, there was no monkey being extracted from his back a la Steve Young. No talk of The Albatross. Reporters tried to roll out that question about validation, confirmation, whatever, and Manning was having none of it.

Good for him, anyway.

That's for the rest of us to consider in our spare time. Right now, he's in the middle of a Hall of Fame career, a Hall of Fame career that had its exclamatory moment Sunday.

"I don't play that card," he said evenly. "I don't play that game."

After all those close calls at the University of Tennessee, all those near-misses with the Colts, there is only one question for Manning, and it won't be asked until long after this team has properly basked in this wonderful result:

"How many will Manning and the Colts win before his career is over?"

The yeah, buts have been expunged from the Manning lexicon. He is a Super Bowl champion. And a Super Bowl MVP, even if Manning quickly acknowledged almost anybody on that team rated MVP mention.

Joseph Addai? Dominic Rhodes? Take your pick.

"Now it's time to party," safety Bob Sanders said boldly. "It's time to let loose."

You think?

Manning wasn't the typically dominant Manning, really couldn't have been with an insistent rain falling. But he didn't have to be, which is why you started to get the sense, especially after that Colts' beat-down in Baltimore in the divisional round, that maybe, yes, it was the Colts' time. Finally.

That's what was so tremendous about this whole championship run. The way this team, which was only supposed to go as far as Manning took them, won over and over again as a team.

All week, the story lines had centered on Dungy and Manning, two men who seemed to have so very much on the line, two men looking to cement their legacies, validate their professional lives — even if neither was inclined to view this game in that fashion. Could Dungy get a team over the hump? Could Manning win The Big One, even if the definition of The Big One kept moving every 10 minutes?

And yet the story of this often strange and sloppy game — this wet game — wasn't necessarily Manning or Dungy, although both played a huge role in this victory. Manning performed a rhapsody in patience. Dungy, cool as always, helped change the course of the game with an important challenge on a Marvin Harrison reception.

The story of this game, though, was the Colts' playoffs-long ability to run the football and stop the run — and the pass, for that matter. They dominated from beginning to end.

Stopping Kansas City's Larry Johnson in his tracks.

Stuffing Baltimore's Jamal Lewis in the angriest road environment you've ever seen.

Coming back from an 18-point deficit, against New England no less, winning the AFC title in style.

And then coming here, to Miami, where it was sunny and gorgeous all week, only to have it rain in sheets. They not only played in Bears weather, they beat their opponent playing Bears football.

A couple of weeks ago, Dungy called one good defensive performance an aberration, two a coincidence and more a pattern.

"I think we've established a pattern," Dungy said with a smile.

They won this championship by doing it the old-fashioned way, by toeing the time-honored philosophical line about what it takes to win in the playoffs.

They ran and they stopped the run.

Simple game, isn't it?

What was remarkable, though, not just in this game but this entire playoff run, is the fact that the Colts essentially redefined themselves when the stakes got highest.

Two months ago, could you have imagined that the Colts' stoutness against the run would mean the difference between an early playoff ouster and a Super Bowl?

They didn't just win this championship; they reinvented themselves. They blew away every long-held stereotype that has attended their ascent into the NFL's elite. Soft? Hardly. Incapable of winning in the elements? No, sir.

"To go through the things we went through, I just feel complete joy," Dungy said. "We may have had better teams in the last couple of five years, but none of them were as ready to win as this. . . . To be able to out-play them at their game says a lot."

This whole remarkable experience — and this will be a remember-when moment for every sports fan in the state — was a testament to the power of faith. One year ago, yes, the Colts were dominant, maybe even better than this championship team, something Dungy suggested after the game. But sometimes, you have to go through more tests.

When it counted most, there was greatness, a champion's mettle. "We imposed our will," Rhodes said proudly.

The rain continued to fall hard as the happy night wore on, soaking everything in its way. But not the Colts' collective joy. And the Lombardi Trophy, the one being shared by Jim Irsay and Dungy and Manning and everybody else on that remarkable team? It had never shone so brightly.

SORRY, BRO

Peyton Manning's Colts defeat Eli's Giants

By Phil Richards

EAST RUTHERFORD, N.J. — In a game billed as the Manning Bowl, brothers Peyton and Eli both made big plays, but the game turned on a big mistake.

Cornerback Nick Harper intercepted an Eli Manning pass with 3:51 to play to help the Indianapolis Colts preserve a 26-21 victory over the New York Giants before a sellout crowd of 78,622 at Giants Stadium.

Colts quarterback Peyton Manning completed 25-of-41 passes for 276 yards and one touchdown with one interception. Little brother Eli hit 20-of-34 attempts for 247 yards and two touchdowns with one interception on a mild, overcast night in the debut of NBC's "Sunday Night Football."

◄ **GOOD GAME:** Indianapolis Colts quarterback Peyton Manning and his brother, Giants quarterback Eli Manning, greet each other after the Colts defeated the Giants. Matt Kryger / The Star

▶ **PICKING HIS TARGET:** Peyton Manning drops back to throw against the Giants in the first quarter. Matt Kryger / The Star

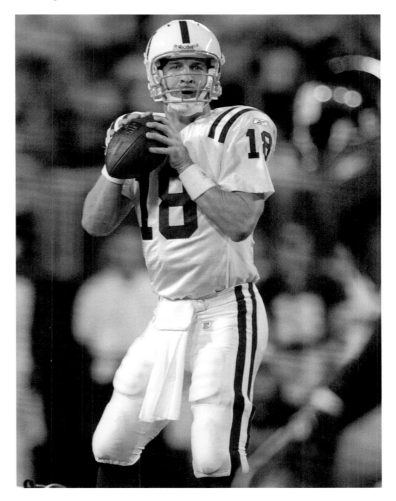

NFL Week One

Colts 26
Giants 21

Team record: 1-0

It was the first time in NFL history that brothers started at quarterback for opposing teams. The Colts' Peyton, 30, is a six-time Pro Bowl player and two-time league MVP. Eli, 25, is a third-year player still learning his craft.

Both are former No. 1 overall draft choices, Peyton in 1998, Eli in 2004.

"It's pretty awesome when you think about it," said Peyton. "If it happens again, I want to meet the two brothers. I don't think it will happen again."

Harper's interception came one play after a controversial offensive pass interference call on Giants wide receiver Tim Carter nullified a first down. The interception set up a 19-yard drive to Adam Vinatieri's fourth field goal in as many attempts.

Vinatieri, an offseason free agent acquisition, hit from 26, 32, 48 and 32 yards.

"Bad decision by me there," Eli said of

▲ **PREGAME CHAT:** Indianapolis Colts quarterback Peyton Manning (left) and his brother, New York Giants quarterback Eli Manning, share a quick chat before the game. **Matt Kryger** / The Star

▶ **GAME FACES:** Indianapolis Colts fans Chris Gregor, 14 (left) and his brother Dan, 10, both from Monroe, N.J., watch the Colts warming up. **Matt Kryger** / The Star

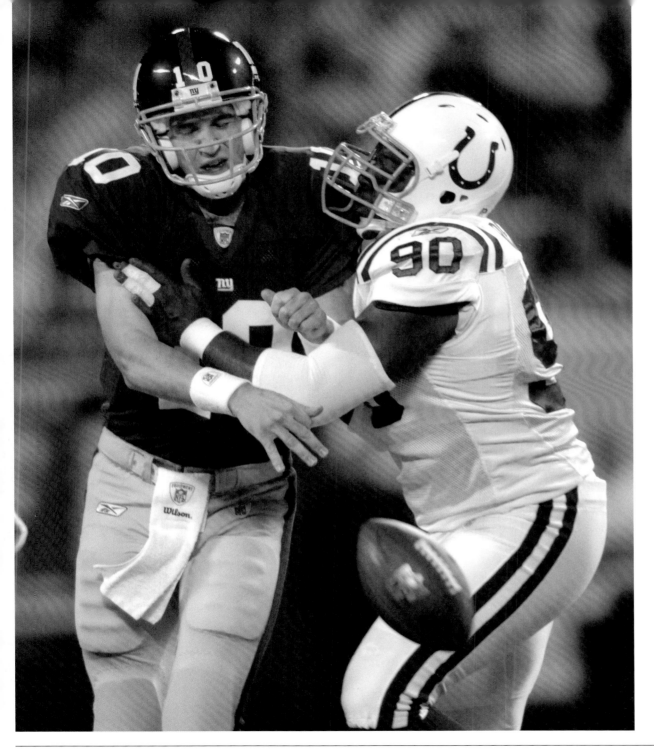

his interception. "We let one slip away a little bit."

Tiki Barber rushed for 110 yards as the Giants outgained the poor-tackling Colts on the ground, 186 yards to 55. New York was 7-1 last season when Barber ran for at least 100 yards.

The Colts got 29 yards on 16 rushes from Dominic Rhodes and 26 yards on seven attempts from rookie Joseph Addai. They averaged 2.4 yards a carry. Rhodes and Addai are replacing Edgerrin James, a four-time Pro Bowl running back who signed with Arizona during the off-season.

"We won. We put some points on the board," Rhodes said. "We've got some kinks we've got to work out."

Colts center Jeff Saturday said a good defense that was set up to take away the run was largely responsible for the running game's problems, but he, too, admitted the obvious.

"We've got a lot of things we need to improve on," Saturday said.

The Colts opened their season on the road for the seventh consecutive year and pushed

◄FEELING THE PRESSURE: New York Giants quarterback Eli Manning gets rid of the ball before he is hit by the Colts' Montae Reagor (90) in the first quarter. Matt Kryger / The Star

their record to 6-1 in those games. They have won 23 of their past 26 regular-season games.

The Colts were penalized only three times for 20 yards. The Giants were flagged 10 times for 64 yards, a factor New York coach Tom Coughlin pointed to as crucial.

He also made it clear that he was no fan of the pass interference call on Carter. It appeared that Harper slipped on the play without being shoved.

"It's very difficult for me to believe a play like that is a foul," Coughlin said.

Had the penalty not been called and the play stood, the Giants would have had a first down at their 37-yard line with 4:03 to play.

Big Bro dominated early. When he threw 2 yards to tight end Dallas Clark for the touchdown that made it 13-0, Peyton was 14-for-24 for 166 yards. Eli was 5-of-10 for 64 yards.

Over the final 2:25 of the first half, each proved he could run the two-minute drill.

Eli was 4-for-5 for 64 yards, including a 34-yard touchdown to wide receiver Plaxico Burris. Harper had good coverage on the play, but the 6-5 Burris used his 7-inch

▶ **GOING FOR MORE:** Dallas Clark of the Colts tries to get extra yards on Antonio Pierce of the Giants during first-quarter action. Robert Scheer / The Star

▶▶ **ROOM TO RUN:** Joseph Addai (29) turns upfield during second-quarter action in Giants Stadium. Robert Scheer / The Star

▼ **RUSHED:** Peyton Manning gets off a pass before he is hit by LaVar Arrington of the Giants in the first quarter. Matt Kryger / The Star

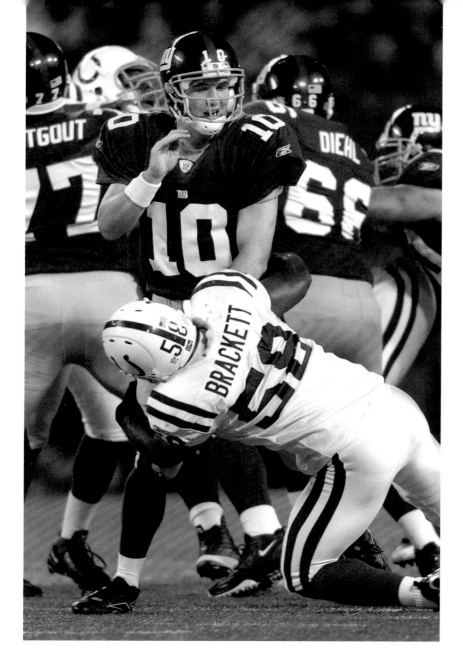

▲ **TAKING A HIT:** Colts linebacker Gary Brackett (58) hits Eli Manning (10) in the second quarter. Matt Kryger / The Star

▶ **IT'S GOOD!:** Colts place-kicker Adam Vinatieri (4) celebrates a 49-yard field goal as time runs out in the first half. Matt Kryger / The Star

height advantage and tipped the ball to himself at the goal line.

Peyton brought the Colts right back. He hit all three of his pass attempts for 30 yards as the Colts maneuvered into position for a 48-yard Vinatieri field goal that made it 16-7 at halftime.

Peyton and Eli met on the field and embraced after the game.

"I said, 'Good game,'" Eli related later. "'Your win. Keep it up.'" ■

▲ **GOING FOR SIX:** Eli Manning fires a touchdown pass to tight end Jeremy Shockey (80) in the third quarter. Matt Kryger / The Star

▶ **EYES UPFIELD:** Colts running back Dominic Rhodes (33) turns upfield in the third quarter. Matt Kryger / The Star

BOB KRAVITZ'S REPORT CARD

D **RUN OFFENSE:** Does anybody else smell a season-long story line developing? Coach Tony Dungy keeps saying the same thing, "Well, defenses are gearing up to stop the run and when they let us run, we'll run effectively." Tell me, can defensive coordinators around the league be so dumb, they'd rather have Peyton Manning throwing to Marvin Harrison instead of getting run on by Dominic Rhodes and Joseph Addai? I'm not the smartest guy — hence, the Dopey Report Card — but if I'm playing the Colts, I'm playing about 14 defensive backs and daring Indy to run.

D **RUN DEFENSE:** Even one day later, it still boggles my mind that Indianapolis could be so utterly ineffective running the ball and stopping the run, and still pull out a quality victory on the road. How many times did we see Dwight Freeney and Robert Mathis fly past the ball carrier? And does Corey Simon make that big a difference? If the Giants don't botch a handoff and commit several penalties, the numbers get real ugly and the Giants likely win that game.

B+ **PASS OFFENSE:** If your name wasn't Manning, you didn't have a snowball's chance to get marquee billing, but Marvin Harrison darn near stole the show. Same with Dallas Clark, who owned the middle of the field and looks poised to have a huge season. Excellent job by the offensive line, keeping the pocket clean against two of the best pass-rushing defensive ends in the league. Oh, and after seeing how quickly Peyton showered, put on a suit and got into the interview room — and the media thank him — I will never question his foot speed again.

B- **PASS DEFENSE:** Interesting night for Nick Harper, huh? At least he didn't get tackled by Eli Manning. You couldn't really blame him for either touchdown. Plaxico Burress is just too tall, and Eli's pass to Jeremy Shockey was just too perfect. And Harper did get a late interception and earned the Reggie Miller Award for Artistic Flopping by drawing that offensive pass interference call against Tim Carter.

A **SPECIAL TEAMS:** Just like we figured: Manning Bowl I would be decided by special teams. OK, that's not how we figured it. The Colts' kickoff coverage team was utterly dominant, the best Dungy has seen in his five years in Indianapolis. It also helped to have a kicker who can reach the goal line instead of the 12 every time. I'm telling you now: Adam Vinatieri is going to have a monster year kicking half his games indoors. And it should be noticed, he played hurt. His predecessor, what's-his-name in Dallas, is nursing his groin.

B **COACHING:** After the game, Dungy said he wouldn't be stubborn and continue to "run uphill" against defensive fronts featuring seven and eight guys in the box, but at some point, soon, the Colts are going to have to make people at least respect the run. Without the run, there's no action in play-action. Another thought: Let's see more of those dump offs to Addai. Maybe an occasional screen. I love telling guys who've been offensive coordinators for 75 years what to do.

A- **INTANGIBLES:** My personal apologies to Hunter Smith, Vice President in Charge of Intangibles, but the late game and the looming deadline made a postgame trip to the locker room impossible. Next week against Houston, he gets two intangibles. Shoot, he can do the whole Dopey Report Card if the spirit moves him.

▲ **SURE EXCHANGE:** Peyton Manning hands off to running back Joseph Addai (29) in the fourth quarter. Matt Kryger / The Star

14

◄**BIG PICK:** Colts defensive back Nick Harper (25) celebrates his interception in the fourth quarter. **Matt Kryger** / The Star

BLUE CRUISES AT DOME

Colts' defensive front sets tone for blowout

By Phil Richards

From the first play from scrimmage Sunday afternoon at the RCA Dome, Houston quarterback David Carr was out to buy time. He took the snap and bootlegged right, away from danger, away from Dwight Freeney, the Indianapolis Colts' Pro Bowl right end.

There was only one problem. It wore No. 98. Left end Robert Mathis hammered Carr for an 8-yard sack and the chase was on.

With their defensive front on the attack, the Colts went off. They splattered the Texans 43-24 to run their record to 2-0 and their AFC South winning streak to 10 games. The Colts have won 24 of their past 27 regular-season games.

"We just tried to get in his face and make him make quick decisions," said Mathis, who had two of the Colts' four sacks.

◄**LISTEN UP!:** The Colts' Peyton Manning yells out instructions from the line of scrimmage during the game. The Colts defeated the Houston Texans 43-24 at the RCA Dome in Indianapolis. **Sam Riche** / The Star

▶**GOOD START:** Colts defensive lineman Robert Mathis sacks Texans quarterback David Carr (left) on the first play of the game. **Matt Kryger** / The Star

NFL Week Two

Colts 43
Texans 24

Team record: 2-0

"Their first option was to bootleg, to get Carr out of the pocket so he could make his reads. They only got one, that first play."

This is the game Colts are designed to play. Get pressure on the quarterback without blitzing. Force hurried decisions and mistakes. Get the football for their lethal offense, get a lead, get the crowd up and in a full roar and get into launch mode.

That's what they did Sunday when the sell-out throng of 56,614 made itself heard. Carr testified to its efficacy.

"Coming up here is a chore because this team feeds off the energy of their crowd, the energy of their stadium, the noise level for their defensive line," he said. "It's hard to put it on the offensive linemen because it's difficult for them when they're

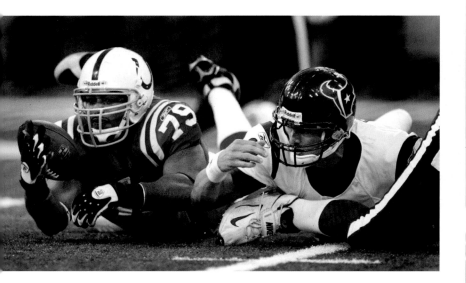

▲ **I'LL TAKE THAT:** The Colts' Raheem Brock grabs this fumble from the Texans' David Carr on the second play of the day. **Sam Riche** / The Star

▶ **PAYDIRT:** Joseph Addai runs by the Texans' Glenn Earl (left) in the first quarter for his first touchdown as a pro. **Matt Kryger** / The Star

keying the defensive end for the snap count. They're watching him as to when to get off the ball, and by the time they do that, he's 3 yards deep."

Carr said it once. Then he repeated himself, and again.

Houston's rebuilt offensive line couldn't hear. It was watching Freeney and Mathis for the snap count. It was beaten before it broke the huddle.

On the second play of the game, center Mike Flanagan couldn't hear the signals. He snapped the football before Carr was ready. By the time the scramble ended and the whistle blew, Colts tackle Raheem Brock, who had 1½ sacks, was cradling the ball at the

▲ **CONGRATULATIONS:** Colts running back Joseph Addai (left) celebrates his first touchdown as a pro and the Colts' second touchdown of the day with teammate Dominic Rhodes in the first quarter. **Matt Detrich** / The Star

▶ **FAMILIAR HOOKUP:** Peyton Manning throws a pass to Reggie Wayne in the second quarter. **Matt Kryger** / The Star

Houston 16-yard line.

Three plays later, the Colts led 7-0. So it went.

With Mathis and Freeney coming off the edges and tackles Brock and Montae Reagor pushing up the middle, Houston (0-2) was forced to abandon its game plan. Down 7-0, then 14-0 and 17-0, it went to an I-formation. It ran the ball and threw short passes off quick drops to its running backs and tight ends.

"The first play of the game shook them up and rattled them," said Reagor, who forced and recovered a fumble. "They had to adjust. We got hits on the quarterback, got sacks. We went into this ballgame with a sense of urgency. We played hard, played fast. We played with a sense of swagger."

Houston has a Pro Bowl receiver on each side; Andre Johnson and Eric Moulds are their most dangerous players. Carr didn't have time

to look for them. He didn't have time to go deep. Johnson and Moulds both caught four passes, but they had a single reception apiece during the first three quarters, before Colts reserves took over on defense.

"That's what we wanted," Colts safety Bob Sanders said. "Our thing was to try to keep a lot of pressure on the quarterback so the ball has to come out quick."

Carr completed 22-of-26 passes for 219 yards

▲ **OUT OF REACH:** Indy's Cato June (59) tries to take down the Texans' Ron Dayne.
Sam Riche / The Star

◀ **FANATIC:** Indianapolis Colts fan Ray Bridges cheers on his team in the second quarter. **Matt Kryger** / The Star

ON THE LOOSE: Colts wide receiver Marvin Harrison runs into the Texans secondary in the third quarter. Matt Kryger / The Star

CLEARING OBSTACLES: Running back Dominic Rhodes jumps over teammate Joseph Addai in the third quarter. Matt Kryger / The Star

▲ **TOUGH RUNNING:** Joseph Addai gets wrapped up by a host of Texans after a gain in first-half action. **Sam Riche** / The Star

▶ **JUST IN TIME:** Peyton Manning gets this pass away just before getting hit by the Texans' N.D. Kalu (94) and Mario Williams (90). **Sam Riche** / The Star

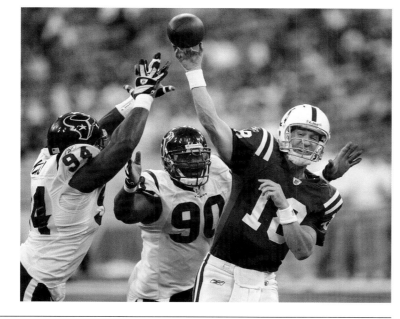

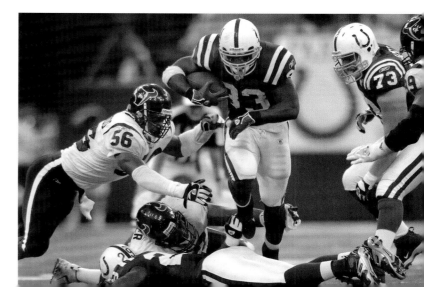

▲ **MILESTONE:** Colts wide receiver Marvin Harrison stiff-arms Texans cornerback Dunta Robinson after hauling in the catch that moved Harrison past Art Monk and into fifth place on the career receptions list. **Matt Detrich** / The Star

▶ **LEFT IN THE DUST:** Harrison burns Texans strong safety Glenn Earl on a route after a catch in the second quarter. **Matt Detrich** / The Star

▼ **FAN CELEBRATION:** Colts fans celebrate Marvin Harrison's milestone reception in the third quarter. **Sam Riche** / The Star

and three touchdowns, but 146 of his yards and all three touchdowns came in the fourth quarter, after the Colts' starters sat down.

The Colts were gouged for 186 rushing yards and a 6.6-yards-per-carry average last week while winning their opener against the New York Giants. The Colts gave up 108 yards on the ground to the Texans, who ran 17 times for 55 yards and a 3.2-yard average over the first three quarters.

"It all starts up front," weakside linebacker Cato June said.

"They made it easy," strongside backer Gilbert Gardner shrugged.

That's the idea. ■

◀**LEAPING GRAB:** Reggie Wayne (right) makes a leaping catch over Texans defensive back Lewis Sanders in the fourth quarter. **Matt Kryger** / The Star

▲ **RUSH! RUSH! RUSH!:** Defensive end Robert Mathis rushes on Texans lineman Zach Wiegert (left) in the third quarter. **Matt Kryger** / The Star

◀**FAN RECOGNITION:** Marvin Harrison points to the crowd after a second-half catch. **Sam Riche** / The Star

BOB KRAVITZ'S REPORT CARD

B **RUN OFFENSE:** Before I start, I've been asked by the one particularly loathsome editor to remind readers the Dopey Report Card is so named as an homage to team president Bill Polian, who likes to rail against pundits and what he calls "their dopey report cards." There. I've explained it unnecessarily to pacify a misguided corporate initiative. Everybody happy? Oh, the running game. It seems the Colts have one. Joseph Addai, meet stardom. Now do it again against Jacksonville and I'll be sold.

B **RUN DEFENSE:** Last week, the Colts' defensive line played as lousy a game as I've seen in a long time. This week, they spent more time in the Texans' backfield than Samkon Gado. The first play of the game, when Dwight Freeney and Robert Mathis met at David Carr's sternum, that set the tone. If there's such a thing as Post Traumatic Sack Syndrome, Carr's going to get it. The stats are misleading. The Texans got 53 of their 108 yards rushing in the fourth quarter.

A− **PASS OFFENSE:** Want some more misleading stats? According to the quarterback-rating calculation, which nobody really understands anyway, Carr had a higher rating Sunday than Peyton Manning. Explain that one to me. Here's the number that matters. The Colts were 9-of-12 in third-down conversions after going 11-of-16 last week against the Giants. You never thought I was a numbers guy, did you? Congratulations, by the way, to Ben Utecht, who somehow remembered his name after taking a brutal hit.

B− **PASS DEFENSE:** Actually, the starters get an A-minus. The subs, who spent the fourth quarter getting torched, get a D. Is it too early to wonder whether Marlin Jackson is a bust? (Answer: No. I mean, it's not too early.) Again, the numbers are as misleading as my expense accounts. Carr was 22-of-26 for 219 yards and three TDs. Big stinking deal.

B+ **SPECIAL TEAMS:** Unbelievable. They went and wore out Adam Vinatieri with all those kickoffs. Now we're hearing he injured his groin. Of course, only his mother knows for sure. Anyway, before he departed the premises, he kicked a touchback, which inspired spasms of pure joy from the assembled masses. As for Hunter the Punter's blocked PAT, let's just say it was the result of a perfect storm of ineptitude. High snap, low kick, no blocking. Oopsie.

A− **COACHING:** I mentioned this in the column, but it is a testament to Tony Dungy, his coaches and his players' professionalism that they never, ever trip over games they're supposed to win. They don't just win, but they get it over within two, three quarters. That said, I'm not quite sure I understood why Manning and the other starters were still out there late in the game, but let's not nit-pick. That wouldn't be in my nature.

A **INTANGIBLES:** From Hunter Smith, Vice President in Charge of Intangibles: "When I was hurt in the preseason, I got to sit in the training room and watch Brandon Stokley rehab his ankle as hard as anybody I've ever seen," Smith said. "He got in for a couple of plays, got a touchdown, and it was totally worth it to him to rehab that hard to come in and jump-start his team, even if he left the game sore. Now that's an intangible."

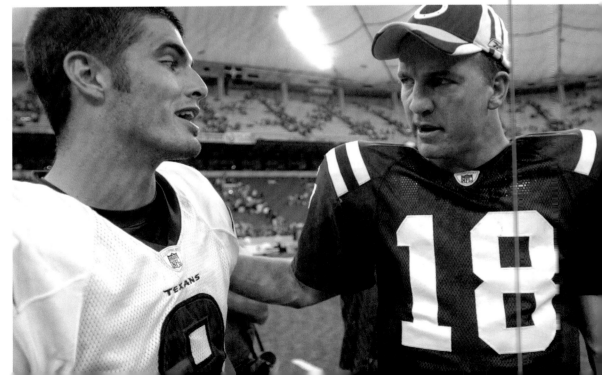

◀ **UPBEAT:** Everyone's all smiles after the Colts defeat the Texans 43-24 at the RCA Dome. **Sam Riche** / The Star

▼ **SEE YOU IN DECEMBER:** Peyton Manning talks to Houston Texans quarterback David Carr at the end of the game.
Matt Kryger / The Star

Addai holds on to this ball

By Phillip B. Wilson

Joseph Addai just plays. He didn't have the foggiest idea his first NFL touchdown made Colts history Sunday. The Houston native just thought he had scored against his hometown team.

The football he caught for that score, however, has just as much meaning, if not more, to the quarterback who threw it.

Sounding like the quiet rookie running back he is, Addai had to be told his 21-yard scoring reception in the first quarter was the 2,797th career completion for quarterback Peyton Manning, surpassing John Unitas' team record.

"Oh, I didn't even know that," Addai said after the Colts' 43-24 home romp over the Texans.

Perhaps this will be another instance where the football needs to be split — remember last season when Manning suggested cutting a ball in half after he and Marvin Harrison became the NFL's all-time TD pass tandem?

"I don't think I'm going to give him that ball," Addai said of his quarterback. "That's for me. That's my first touchdown. I won't never forget that one."

Manning knows the drill. He hasn't had much luck retrieving special footballs from his pass catchers. He made light of trying in vain in the past to snag a touchdown ball as a keepsake from Harrison or Reggie Wayne.

"Marvin and Reggie, don't even think about that. Marvin and Reggie, that ball is already locked and secured," he said. "As soon as it leaves my hands, I guess it's no longer my property."

What probably mattered more to Manning was how Addai handled himself in his second pro game. The quarterback reminded it's not always about knowing when to block but when not to block.

Addai was supposed to block on the play in which he scored. With nobody to block, he slipped through the line and was open. After two Texans ran into each other, his angle to the end zone was wide open.

"I was just trying to get to the pylon," he said.

If he does that enough, he may end up getting the starting job from Dominic Rhodes. Not that the Colts are concerning themselves with who starts — they're both going to get their share of work.

But strictly on stats, Addai outplayed Rhodes for the second consecutive week. Addai ran 16 times for 82 yards, a 5.1 average. Rhodes gained 37 yards on 14 carries, 2.6 per carry. Each caught two passes for 22 yards.

Not that Addai was perfect. He lost a goal-line fumble. But other than that, Addai had a productive game. Surrounded later by media at his locker, he unselfishly downplayed whether he or Rhodes should ultimately get most of the carries.

"I can't really say," Addai said. "I don't know the situation. I just go into it like whenever I get my opportunity, I take advantage of it. That's the same thing I did in college and I got an opportunity to get to the next level, so I'm going to keep doing the same thing."

Rhodes said some have suggested there's a rift between the two but insisted it's untrue.

For one moment in the locker room, it looked as if Rhodes was representing for the rookie. Rhodes wore a No. 29 Colts jersey, the number Addai wears. But the name on the back read, "Dickerson," in honor of Hall of Fame back Eric Dickerson.

Rhodes said he would gladly wear Addai's jersey, too.

▲ **HIS FIRST TD:** Colts running back Joseph Addai (right) celebrates his first-quarter touchdown with Dominic Rhodes. **Matt Kryger** / The Star

"He could wear my jersey and I would wear his jersey," he said. "It's the Rhodes-Addai show or the Addai-Rhodes show, whatever it is."

POISE PAYS

Colts win on Doss' big plays, team's patience

By Phil Richards

Mike Doss missed most of the preseason with a strained left calf muscle. He lost his starting spot to rookie safety Antoine Bethea. He walked the sideline. He played sparingly.

He maintained his poise and patience.

"In this game, you've got to be patient. It's a long season," said Doss, who got his chance Sunday and energized the defense with some big second-half hits and a crucial final-minute interception as the Indianapolis Colts dumped AFC South rival Jacksonville 21-14 at the RCA Dome.

The Colts (3-0) were a study in poise and patience while moving a game ahead of the Jaguars (2-1). Maturity carried the day.

NFL Week Three

Colts 21
Jaguars 14

Team record: 3-0

◀ **STOP SIGN:** Colts defensive back Mike Doss (20) puts a jarring stop to Jacksonville tight end George Wrighster, leaving him short of a first down in the third quarter against the Jacksonville Jaguars. Matt Detrich / The Star

▶ **LOOKING FOR AN ANGLE:** The Colts' Terrence Wilkins heads upfield on a punt return against the Jags' Gerald Sensabaugh in second-half action. Sam Riche / The Star

PREGAME RITUAL: Peyton Manning, top, and running back Dominic Rhodes run through a line of fellow players as they take the field against Jacksonville. **Mike Fender** / The Star

GETTING PHYSICAL: Colts linebacker Gary Brackett (58) loses his helmet after tackling Fred Taylor (28) in the second quarter. Cato June (59) and Robert Mathis, rear, (98) assist on the tackle. **Matt Kryger** / The Star

GAME-CHANGER: Terrence Wilkins runs back a punt for a touchdown in the second quarter. **Matt Kryger** / The Star

Jacksonville dominated the first half. The Jaguars broke tackles, piled up a 157-10 advantage in rushing yards and held the football for 24 minutes, 31 seconds to the Colts' 5:29. The Colts had a 51-yard Peyton Manning-to-Reggie Wayne completion overturned on a controversial call. Twice Jaguars cornerback Rashean Mathis appeared to interfere with Colts wide receiver Marvin Harrison on what might have been touchdown passes. Neither drew a flag.

The Colts didn't blink. They just kept playing.

"You do have to stay poised," said Manning, who completed 14-of-31 passes for 219 yards and a touchdown against

▲ **OUT OF REACH:** Colts wide receiver Marvin Harrison just misses catching the ball in the second quarter. Matt Kryger / The Star

▶ **LET'S TALK:** Colts coach Tony Dungy calls a timeout in second half action. Sam Riche / The Star

▶▶ **HE'S THE MAN:** Linebacker Cato June celebrates after teammate Mike Doss stops Jacksonville tight end George Wrighster short of a first down in the third quarter. Matt Detrich / The Star

Jacksonville's big, strong, brutally competitive defense. "Offensively we've been in enough games and guys have been around enough to know that it's going to be a four-quarter game and you've got to move on from it."

The defense did the same as the Colts won their 11th consecutive AFC South game and for the 25th time in their past 28 regular-season games. After missing tackles in bunches and yielding 5 yards a snap during the first half, they tightened down and permitted 3.5 yards a play during the second.

While Jacksonville was losing its poise and committing unsportsman-like conduct and unnecessary roughness penalties, the Colts just played.

That's one reason they're 7-2 against the emotionally fragile Jaguars since realignment established the AFC South in 2002.

The Colts played turnover-free football. Jags quarterback Byron Leftwich pitched a pair of interceptions. Place-kicker Josh Scobee, who kicked a 53-yard

◀SACK: Colts defensive linemen Raheem Brock (79) and Robert Mathis (98) sack Byron Leftwich in the third quarter. Matt Kryger / The Star

◀◀NICE CATCH: Colts tight end Dallas Clark (44) celebrates a touchdown with Jake Scott (73) and Dylan Gandy in the third quarter.
Matt Kryger / The Star

field goal with 38 seconds to play to beat the Colts 27-24 at the RCA Dome in 2004, missed Sunday from 24 and 49 yards.

"You have to give them credit more so than anything. They were the better team today, more discipline," said Jacksonville running back Fred Taylor.

The Colts had every reason to panic, but no inclination to.

They got virtually nothing right offensively or defensively during the first half but repaired to the locker room with a 7-7 tie because of Terrence Wilkins' 82-yard punt return for a touchdown.

They emerged after halftime, took the opening kickoff and clicked off seven plays, the last a 30-yard Manning pass to tight end Dallas Clark for a 14-7 lead. The 80-yard drive exceeded their first-half output by 14 yards.

"When you play a great defense like they've got, you just keep grinding and don't let it frustrate you," said Colts right guard Jake Scott. "If you let it frustrate you, you're going to start making mistakes. If you keep grinding, eventually something good is going to happen."

Doss and the defense also stepped up. On

▲ **THAT'S MY BALL!:** Reggie Wayne hauls in this fourth-quarter pass at the 3-yard line against the Jags' Donovin Darius. Sam Riche / The Star

its second third-quarter play, Doss took Taylor down for no gain. Doss has had his problems in coverage, but he has never been a bashful hitter. On third-and-6, he hammered tight end George Wrighster to the turf after 3 yards on a reception from Leftwich.

"Mike had a big hit," said Gary Brackett, the Colts' middle linebacker and defensive captain. "I think that kind of lit a fire under us."

Doss' biggest play came with 57 seconds remaining. On second-and-10 from the Colts 42, Jacksonville wide receiver Reggie Williams lined up in the slot and ran the left hash marks. Doss was playing deep in the Colts' cover-2 alignment. He knew the Jaguars would try to go long. He read Leftwich, broke on the football and made the clinching interception.

"I'm just glad to be back," said Doss, who started because Pro Bowl safety Bob Sanders was out with a sore knee and made nine tackles. "To come back this way is just a blessing."

Patience paid. ■

▲ **THE GREAT RUNNER:** Colts quarterback Peyton Manning, on a bootleg, jogs into the end zone for a touchdown in the fourth quarter. **Matt Kryger** / The Star

▶ **NICE RUN:** Manning is all smiles while celebrating his touchdown with teammates in the fourth quarter. **Matt Detrich** / The Star

◀ **ELATION:** Colts quarterback Peyton Manning is congratulated by an elated backup quarterback Jim Sorgi after Manning ran the ball in for a touchdown in the fourth quarter. **Matt Detrich** / The Star

◀ **BIG PICK:** Indy's Mike Doss, center, celebrates with his teammates on the sideline after intercepting the Jags' Byron Leftwich to seal the victory in the final minutes. Sam Riche / The Star

▼ **THAT WAY!:** Doss signals a change in possession after his interception.
Sam Riche / The Star

BOB KRAVITZ'S REPORT CARD

D **RUN OFFENSE:** It's not like Edgerrin James is tearing it up for Arizona, either, so it could be worse. But the Colts should consider themselves very fortunate, winning two of their games without anything resembling a running attack. By the third quarter, they just gave up trying. If this doesn't improve, the Colts are a playoff disaster waiting to happen. I'm just warning you now.

B- **PASS OFFENSE:** When you consider they had absolutely no running game, or threat of a running game, Manning and Co. did a pretty decent job getting anything accomplished. Remember, this Jacksonville front four is able to get pressure on the quarterback, and the rest of the defenders drop into coverage. This just wasn't going to be a big-numbers kind of day. But playmakers make plays. Reggie Wayne. Marvin Harrison. Dallas Clark (although I could have caught that pass). And Manning, of course.

C **RUN DEFENSE:** Basically, that's an F for the first half, and an A for the second half. The first half, the tackling was abysmal, laughable almost. Fred Taylor and Maurice Jones-Drew would get the ball, stutter step and wait for defenders to commit, then bounce it outside and leave would-be tacklers in their wake. Give them credit, though. Even without Bob Sanders and Corey Simon in the lineup, the Colts defenders found a second wind and stuffed the run in the second half.

A **PASS DEFENSE:** The Colts didn't have Sanders. And early in the game, they lost Nick Harper. So we saw a lot of Mike Doss. We saw a lot of Marlin Jackson. And we saw very little of the Jaguars' passing game. Byron Leftwich threw for just 107 yards and was intercepted twice. I'm not suggesting he's the forgotten Manning brother or anything, but you hold any NFL quarterback to those numbers, you've done a job.

A **SPECIAL TEAMS:** So you go into the most important game of the season so far, you don't have Adam Vinatieri, and you walk out of it winning the special teams battle by a mile. Go figure. All Terrence Wilkins' punt return did was save the game for the Colts. Martin Gramatica? He didn't have a field goal attempt. But by doing nothing, he outplayed Jacksonville's Josh Scobee, who had a nightmare game. I just can't believe they didn't give Dave Rayner a call.

B **COACHING:** Maybe I'm just sensitive after watching the coaching clinics put on Saturday by Minnesota's Glen Mason and Michigan State's John L. Smith, but this made me crazy. Colts ball, third-and-6 at their own 27, 1:55 remaining in the game. With a chance to put away the game, wouldn't you rather give Peyton and his receivers a chance, than hand off to Dominic Rhodes and likely leave the game in the hands of the defense? I understand: The Jaguars were out of timeouts. Hey, what good is a columnist if he can't second-guess?

A **INTANGIBLES:** From Hunter Smith, Vice President in Charge of Intangibles (and Jacksonville, you're going to love this): "Jacksonville is like the stand-up comic who can only use vulgarity and curse words because he lacks intelligence and lacks class. He really doesn't have anything to say. Our intangible is our class and our intelligence. A team that gets personal fouls the way they do, the roughing penalties, they just don't have any material.''

▶**IT'S YOU:** Colts wide receiver Reggie Wayne smiles and points to the fans after the Colts' 21-14 win over the Jacksonville Jaguars. **Matt Kryger** / The Star

▲**FEELS SO GOOD:** Dallas Clark celebrates the victory. **Sam Riche** / The Star

▶**GOOD GAME:** Colts coach Tony Dungy (left) and Jaguars coach Jack Del Rio shake shands following the game. **Matt Kryger** / The Star

Defense returns to the basics

By Mike Chappell

On the verge of being run out of their own building Sunday, the Indianapolis Colts' defense retreated to the locker room at halftime. It regrouped, adjusted.

Voila. After being gored for 154 first-half yards by Jacksonville's one-two punch of running backs Fred Taylor and Maurice Jones-Drew, the Colts tightened the screws considerably. They were more disciplined with their assignments, better at swarming and tackling. It was a major reason the Colts wrestled a 21-14 victory from the Jaguars.

"We talked about it at halftime and got it settled down a little bit," coach Tony Dungy said.

Over the final two quarters, Jacksonville's once-lethal running game was neutralized: 34 yards on 11 carries.

What was the snazzy alteration? Basically, it was going back to playing basic defense. That started with better tackling.

"We came in (at halftime) and made some adjustments. We just slowed some things down," tackle Montae Reagor said. "We said, 'Let's play it straight up.' We said, 'Everyone play your gap; don't fast-flow to the ball. Play the cutback because that's what the back's looking for.'

"It was a minor adjustment that paid off for us."

Too often in the first half, the Colts' aggressive defenders either failed to secure a gap, which led to a gashing run, or over-pursued, which allowed Taylor and Jones-Drew to cut back and break off huge gains. Jones-Drew, a 5-7 rookie out of UCLA who blends power with speed and shiftiness, finished with a career-high 103 yards. He had 87 on eight first-half carries that included runs of 26, 18, 12 and 11 yards.

"He's a guy you've got to hit and wrap up," Dungy said of Jones-Drew. "He ran through us quite a bit in the first half."

So the Jaguars kept running it.

"They weren't stopping the run," quarterback Byron Leftwich said. "They couldn't stop it, so we decided we'll keep running the ball."

That changed after the break. Jacksonville's longest run in the second half was 7 yards by Leftwich. Jones-Drew's longest was 6 yards.

Once they sealed the cutback lanes, the Colts focused on finishing plays with secure tackles.

"It's simple football," Pro Bowl linebacker Cato June said. "If you don't tackle, you make it tough to win. If you do tackle, you can have a lot of fun."

Jacksonville dominated virtually every phase in the first half: 37-18 in plays, 13-3 in first downs, 24 minutes, 31 seconds to 5:29 in possession time. Credit its ability to run through the Colts' defense.

Once the Colts took away the Jaguars' legs, the game's momentum swung. Jacksonville was limited to 112 total yards on 32 plays in the second half.

On the Jaguars' first possession of the third quarter, safety Mike Doss sliced into the backfield and cut down Taylor for no gain on second-and-6. On third

▲ **DON'T LET GO:** Colts linebacker Cato June (59) gets a grip on Jacksonville running back Maurice Jones-Drew. The Indianapolis defense had a problem tackling the Jaguars' ball carriers in the first half. They gained 157 rushing yards before halftime. **Matt Kryger / The Star**

down, he limited tight end George Wrighster to a 3-yard gain with a forceful face-to-face hit, forcing a punt.

Later in the half, June stopped Jones-Drew for a 1-yard gain, then for no gain.

"In the end, we just started playing some good defense," linebacker Gary Brackett said. "We started making some tackles.

"It was going back to basic defense, doing what we do. Just line up and play."

Anything else?

"We tackled better," Brackett said.

GREAT ESCAPE

Manning's magic helps Colts withstand mistakes

By Mike Chappell

EAST RUTHERFORD, N.J. — Coach Tony Dungy was impressed, not in awe, after watching Peyton Manning's latest fourth-quarter heroics Sunday at the Meadowlands.

But Dungy's displeasure was palpable nonetheless as his quarterback and supporting cast had to score two touchdowns in the final 2 minutes, 34 seconds before the Indianapolis Colts could secure a 31-28 victory over the New York Jets.

"We expect that," Dungy said after Manning drove the Colts through the Jets defense for 12-play and nine-play drives to thwart the Jets' upset bid. "We practice that all the time ... so it didn't surprise anybody in our locker room that we were able to do that."

Dungy paused. His eyes revealed the irritation of a

◀LAST MINUTE HEROICS: Peyton Manning drops back to pass in the fourth quarter of the Colts' 31-28 win over the New York Jets at Giants Stadium in East Rutherford, N.J. Matt Kryger / The Star

▶LOOKING FOR A HOLE: Colts running back Joseph Addai looks upfield against the Jets defense in the third quarter. Matt Kryger / The Star

NFL Week Four

Colts 31
Jets 28

Team record: 4-0

coach who was happy with a victory that enabled the Colts to push their record to 4-0 for the third time in four seasons and just the eighth time in franchise history, but not with the manner it was achieved.

"You shouldn't have to do it twice in a game," he said.

That's precisely what was required, though.

Too many penalties — 10 in all from a team that annually ranks among the NFL's least penalized.

"That's absurd," Dungy said.

And then there was a 103-yard kickoff return by New York's Justin Miller — the longest in Jets

▲ **STREET BALL:** Colts fan Ryan Crossan catches a football in front of Jets fan and his brother Dylan Crossan as Giants fan Ryan Murphy (left) watches before the game.
Matt Kryger / The Star

◀ **THOUGHTFUL FAN:** Colts fan Kate Frederick-Kane, Albany, N.Y., holds a sign for Colts wide receiver Reggie Wayne, whose brother died in a car accident last week.
Matt Kryger / The Star

◀◀ **FAMILY DISPUTE:** Colts fan Michael Chiapperino, 9, Blauvelt, N.Y., roughs up his brother Tommy, 7, a Jets fan, as they play before the game. **Matt Kryger** / The Star

▲ **LOOSE BALL:** Colts defensive lineman Robert Mathis (98) knocks the ball loose from New York Jets quarterback Chad Pennington, causing a fumble in the first quarter. **Matt Kryger** / The Star

▲ **VICTORY DANCE:** Colts running back Dominic Rhodes celebrates his touchdown in the first quarter. **Matt Kryger** / The Star

▶ **SACK CELEBRATION:** Colts defensive lineman Montae Reagor (90) celebrates a sack with Robert Mathis in the second quarter.
Matt Kryger / The Star

history and the longest ever allowed by the Colts — that came with 2:20 remaining and trumped Manning's first comeback drive.

No sooner had Manning given the Colts a 24-21 lead with 2:34 left with a 2-yard touchdown pass to tight end Bryan Fletcher than he had to reload. Down 28-24 following Miller's dramatic return, Manning, once and for all, registered the 24th game-winning drive of his career.

"There truly was never any panic," he said. "When they ran that kickoff back, it can be deflating, but only if it's the last play of the game."

It wasn't. Two minutes, 15 seconds remained when Manning stepped behind center Jeff Saturday. No time-outs? No worry.

Manning completed 6-of-8 passes for 60 yards on the drive, including a

▲**BROKEN UP:** Mike Doss (20) and Kelvin Hayden (26) break up a pass intended for Laveranues Coles in the third quarter. **Matt Kryger** / The Star

◀**UPENDED:** Doss (20) upends the Jets' Cedric Houston (34) as Gary Brackett (rear) assists on the tackle in the third quarter. **Matt Kryger** / The Star

▶**PICK:** Linebacker Rocky Boiman (50) intercepts a Chad Pennington pass in the end zone on a fourth-and-2 play in front of the Jets' James Dearth (85) in the third quarter. **Matt Kryger** / The Star

19-yarder to Marvin Harrison on third-and-6 from the Jets 35 and a 15-yarder to Reggie Wayne that produced a first-and-goal at the 1 with 1:13 remaining. On the next play, Manning followed Saturday into the end zone on a sneak.

"One of Jeff's favorite plays," Manning said.

Manning pulled himself out of the pile of humanity, ran to the back of the end zone and spiked the football. Consider it an exclamation mark on a difficult day at the office.

Nothing came easy as Jets quarterback Chad Pennington completed 17-of-23 passes for 207 yards and a 33-yard touchdown to Jerricho Cotchery. He ran a quicker version of the Colts' no-huddle that limited Indy's defensive substitutions and forced it to exhaust its timeouts midway through the fourth quarter. Also, New York's 27th-ranked ground game even came alive with 135 yards.

▲ **YOU MISSED THE CALL!:** Colts coach Tony Dungy has a few words for field judge Scott Edwards in the third quarter. **Matt Kryger** / The Star

▶ **RUNNING DOWNHILL:** Colts running back Joseph Addai (29) runs into the Jets defense in the third quarter. **Matt Kryger** / The Star

And then there were the Colts' self-inflicted wounds.

"I told the team in the locker room we were very fortunate to win," Dungy said. "The one good thing I like about our team is we know how to win and we play hard for 60 minutes. We seem to find a way to win these games."

However, he added, "we talked about the things that we need to do and we didn't do many of them. Had a lot of penalties, the kick return, the onside kick (recovered by the Jets), a lot of things that can cost you a game, and will cost us a game down the road if we're not careful."

Veteran running back Dominic Rhodes teamed with rookie Joseph Addai as the Colts piled up a season-high 160 yards on the ground. Rhodes insisted no one should have been surprised that Manning was able to rescue the Colts, even if it required him doing it twice.

"It's never over," Rhodes said. "As long as we've got time on the clock, we know we can come back and win games. We persevere." ■

▶ **GOOD FOR SIX:** Tight end Bryan Fletcher scores a touchdown in front of Jets defensive back Kerry Rhodes (25) in the fourth quarter.
Matt Kryger / The Star

▶▶ **STAYIN' ALIVE:** Colts wide receiver Marvin Harrison hauls in a Peyton Manning pass for 19 yards with 1:19 to play to keep alive the winning touchdown drive.
Matt Detrich / The Star)

▲ **TURNING A DEAF EAR:** Peyton Manning gets an earful from the Jets fans after the game. Matt Kryger / The Star

◄ **SNEAKING IN:** Peyton Manning barges into the end zone behind center Jeff Saturday (63) for the winning touchdown. It came on a 1-yard sneak with 50 seconds left. Matt Kryger / The Star

▼ **WORDS BETWEEN QUARTERBACKS:** Peyton Manning (right) and Chad Pennington greet each other following the game. Matt Kryger / The Star

BOB KRAVITZ'S REPORT CARD

A‑ **RUN OFFENSE:** Edge Who? Sorry. I'm not trying to be disrespectful. But this is what the Colts imagined when they decided they couldn't sink mega-millions into Edgerrin James and chose to go with the two-headed monster. For the first time this season, a defense played the Colts the way we expected teams to play them, putting a mass of humanity into pass coverage and daring them to run. The Colts took them up on the offer.

B **PASS OFFENSE:** I'm looking back at my notes here: "First quarter, Colts net minus-13 yards passing." And "Manning, first half, 6-of-10 for 77. When did he become Trent Dilfer?" And, "What is wrong with this pass offense? Who are these people?" And then came the fourth quarter. And those two drives. And all is well again.

C **RUN DEFENSE:** Yeah, this is officially An Issue. Four games isn't a blip on the radar, an aberration; it's a trend, and it's not a particularly good one. The Jets were averaging 2.6 yards per carry coming into this game, and after they spent the first quarter struggling to so much as reach the line of scrimmage, they started gashing the Colts as the game wore on. Is all of this a function of Corey Simon's absence? Bob Sanders' absence? Does size matter? You would hope that by December, this wouldn't be An Issue anymore. I'm betting it will be.

B **PASS DEFENSE:** At the risk of sounding like an alarmist — no, not me — I'm going to mention that Dwight Freeney doesn't have any sacks yet this season. That's not to say he's been lousy or anything, but if you're in a contract year, and you want to be the highest-paid defensive player in the game, and you're basically paid to sack the quarterback, this is not the way to do your business. Or so Drew Rosenhaus once told me over a capuccino. Otherwise, pretty solid job by a patched-up secondary.

F **SPECIAL TEAMS:** If you're keeping score at home, there were special teams penalties, an onside kick (hey, look out for the onside kick!!!), Terrence Wilkins' muffed kick return and a bunch of miserably short kickoffs that killed the Colts in field position and left me pining for Dave Rayner. And, of course, there was Martin Gramatica's one good kickoff, which resulted in Justin Miller's 103-yard kickoff return. If I'm the Colts, I'm finding the doctors who fixed Chad Pennington and I'm immediately putting them on Adam Vinatieri's case.

C **COACHING:** After the game, the normally imperturbable Tony Dungy was very upset about the defensive substitution problems that forced his team to blow all their timeouts. Frankly, I would be upset at how ill-prepared the Colts looked to handle the Jets' no-huddle, which they've been running the first three games of the season. It was like they were getting a taste of their own medicine. On the other hand, Dungy didn't go for it on fourth-and-goal at the 2-yard line, which made him the smartest guy at the Meadowlands. Seriously, was Eric Mangini channeling his inner Charlie Weis?

INC. **INTANGIBLES:** Well, this can't be good. I looked everywhere for Hunter Smith, Vice President in Charge of Intangibles and part-time Colts punter, and he was nowhere to be found. There were rumors that after last week's unfortunate slip of the tongue — c'mon, it was funny — he'd become inconsolable and had accidentally overdosed on Flintstones chewables. I will follow up on this and keep you informed.

✓ UNDEFEATED
✓ UNCONVINCING

By Phil Richards

Wide receiver Reggie Wayne spent the last few minutes before kickoff inciting the RCA Dome crowd. He waved a towel and led cheers in the west end zone, then jogged the sideline, exhorting fans all the way to the other end of the field, where the chant rose: "Reggie. Reggie. Reggie."

Wayne had given them nothing to shout about yet. He caught a 2-yard pass with 5:10 to play for the decisive touchdown as the Indianapolis Colts beat Tennessee 14-13. This time, the sell-out crowd of 57,021 rose and roared.

It was a roar of elation. It was a roar of relief. Tennessee (0-5) was an 18½-point underdog.

"It's like we used to say when we were in college," Wayne offered. "Those guys are on scholarship, too."

◀**YES!:** Colts receiver Reggie Wayne (87) celebrates his winning TD catch.
Sam Riche / The Star

▶**COLTS PRIDE:** Indy fans show their support during the last quarter. Sam Riche / The Star

NFL Week Five

Colts 14
Titans 13

Team record: 5-0

▲ **TEAM COLORS:** Colts fans Bud Conklin, Frankfort, Ind., shows off his painted head before the game. **Matt Kryger** / The Star

◄ **GRAND ENTRANCE:** The Colts take the field at the RCA Dome behind their mascot Blue. **Mike Fender** / The Star

▼ **TAKE-DOWN:** Blue takes out the Titans mascot during pregame festivities. **Sam Riche** / The Star

Wayne hadn't caught a touchdown pass all season. Neither had wide receiver Marvin Harrison. They accounted for both touchdowns on a day the Colts (5-0) needed everything they had to win their 12th consecutive AFC South game and maintain a two-game lead on Jacksonville.

The Titans, no doubt, left muttering. Some of the crowd probably did, also. Not the Colts.

"You can't be mad at a win," said cornerback Nick Harper, "no matter how you get it."

Tennessee trampled the Colts during the first half. The Titans rushed for 152 yards and took a 10-0 lead. The Colts offense got no traction. It couldn't stay on the field.

Things turned around during the second half. The Colts defense yielded 86 yards and three points. The offense accumulated 201 yards and 14 points. It made plays.

Wayne connected with quarterback Peyton Manning on a couple of them.

After Harrison caught a 13-yard touchdown pass to punctuate a 90-yard third-quarter drive, Wayne had a chance. On second-and-8 from the

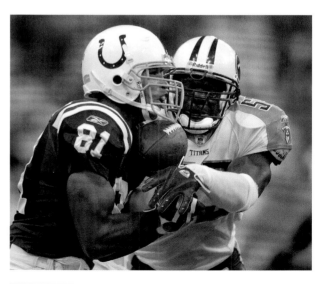

◀**LOOKING FOR A TARGET:** Peyton Manning drops back to throw in the second quarter. Matt Kryger / The Star

▼ **BREAKUP:** Titans linebacker Keith Bulluck (right) breaks up a pass intended for Colts tight end Bryan Fletcher in the first quarter. Matt Kryger / The Star

Tennessee 10, a Manning pass came in hot, went through Wayne's hands and was intercepted by safety Chris Hope.

"A missile," Wayne called it.

Manning kept going to him.

On third-and-8 at the Titans 41 with 8:58 to play and the Colts' opportunities obviously numbered, Wayne was the man. He lined up in the slot, ran an out and made a laid-out catch for 12 yards and a first down.

"You go back and you say that was probably the pivotal play of the game . . . ," said Manning, who completed 20-of-31 passes for 166 yards. "Reggie got double-coverage with the safety over the top and (cornerback Cortland Finnegan) had tight coverage, but Reggie's made that diving catch a lot."

Seven plays later, on third-and-goal, Manning returned to Wayne for the winning touchdown.

It wasn't over until Tennessee's last desperate play on a day that sent practically everyone home drained. No one had more reason to be than Wayne, who was wired from

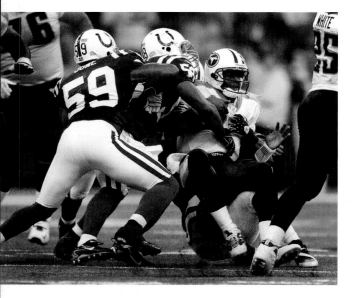

▲ **TURNING UP THE PRESSURE:** Colts Cato June (59) and Gary Brackett tackle Titans quarterback Vince Young in the second quarter. Matt Kryger / The Star

▶ **TOUCHDOWN:** Colts wide receiver Marvin Harrison (88) catches a touchdown pass in front of Titans cornerback Andre Woolfolk (26) in the third quarter. Matt Kryger / The Star

▶▶ **GAINING GROUND:** Dominic Rhodes is brought down by Keith Bulluck of the Titans on this fourth quarter play. Robert Scheer / The Star

pregame to the end.

"I'm emotional every game," Wayne shrugged. "I've been dreaming this since I was a little kid, since I was 7 years old. So playing in front of a big crowd and being out there having fun is an awesome feeling."

Later, Wayne admitted that he might have brought a little greater depth of sentiment than usual that Sunday. His brother, Rashad, 32, was killed in a traffic accident Sept. 24.

After his touchdown catch, Reggie was knocked out of the end zone by Titans safety Lamont Thompson. Wayne gathered himself and walked back into the end zone. He knelt on one knee and raised his index finger toward the sky.

It was the most private of moments amidst 57,000 in full scream. ■

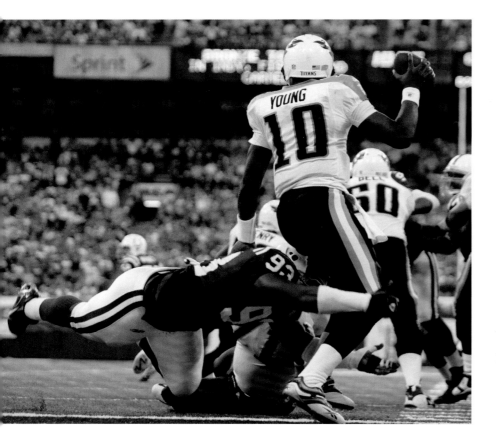

▲ **MORE PRESSURE:** Dwight Freeney pressures Vince Young of the Titans during fourth-quarter action. Robert Scheer/ The Star

▶**SCRAMBLING:** Titans quarterback Vince Young (10) scrambles out of the pocket late in the fourth quarter against the Colts' Raheem Brock. Sam Riche/ The Star

SANDWICHED: Indy's Brandon Stokley is sandwiched on this second-half reception between Titans David Thornton (50) and Keith Bullock (53). Stokley had one more catch, then left the game with a leg injury. **Sam Riche/** The Star

GAME-WINNER: Reggie Wayne (87) scores a fourth-quarter touchdown as Lamont Thompson defends for the Titans. **Robert Scheer/** The Star

KRAVITZ ON THE COLTS

I believe they're bored.

That's right.

Bored.

And frankly, I can't say I blame them.

Let's be honest: No matter how hard this team works, no matter how professional they are, no matter how many leaders they have doing and saying the right things, these players know, way deep down, their ultimate legacy will be written in January.

Remember, they dusted everybody two years ago, watched Peyton Manning throw a record 49 touchdown passes. And lost to New England in the playoffs. Regular season? What regular season?

Last year, they dusted everybody, not only won their first 13 games, but won all of them by at least seven points. Then they lost to Pittsburgh in the playoffs. Regular season? What regular season?

The Colts, I sense now, are on cruise control. Just doing enough to win. Just interested enough to beat the teams they're supposed to beat.

BIG THANKS: Indy's Montae Reagor waves to the crowd after the win. **Sam Riche/** The Star

53

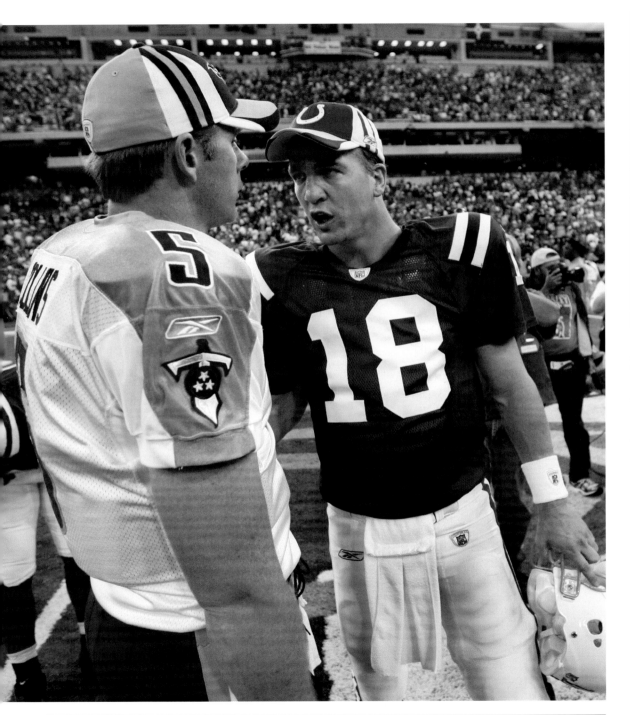

▲ **NUMBER ONE:** Jason David of the Colts signals to the fans after their 4-13 win over the Titans. **Matt Kryger** / The Star

◄ **MAYBE NEXT TIME:** Peyton Manning chats with Kerry Collins, backup quarterback for the Titans, after the game. **Robert Scheer** / The Star

▼ **MANNING FANS:** Colts fans Kim Aker (left) Jennifer Revell (center) and Angela Altherr hold their Peyton Manning masks from one of his popular television commercials. **Matt Kryger** / The Star

Run defense flattened again

By Mike Chappell

Montae Reagor is mad as hell and doesn't want to take it anymore.

Take what? Take getting the football run down the collective throat of the Indianapolis Colts defense.

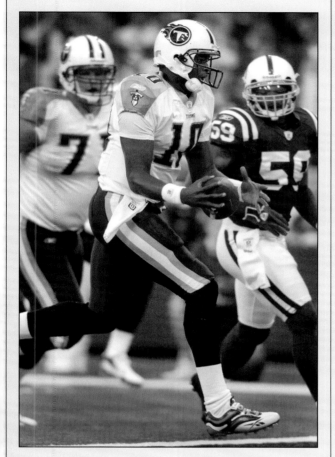

ON THE LOOSE: Titans quarterback Vince Young runs 19 yards into the end zone for his team's first score. Colts defenders couldn't stop the run during the first half. Matt Kryger / The Star

It was deja vu all over again Sunday in the RCA Dome.

Yes, the Colts remained one of the league's three unbeatens with a 14-13 win over the winless Tennessee Titans. But for the fourth time in five games, the defense was gouged for humongous yardage on the ground. The Titans, averaging a sickly 70.3 rushing yards in their first four games, got well at the Colts' expense: 214 yards on 31 carries.

"It's us," Reagor said, his anger evident. "It's our defense. We've got to quit missing tackles and start making the tackles we're supposed to make.

"We have to."

They didn't against the Titans. Travis Henry popped 'em for 123 yards on 19 carries. It was his 12th career 100-yard game but first since December 2003. Rookie LenDale White needed only eight carries to generate 48 yards. Rookie quarterback Vince Young added 43 yards on four carries, including a 19-yard touchdown.

Incredibly, of the Titans' 31 rushes, 10 picked up at least 10 yards. That's been a persistent problem. The Colts now have been gashed for 25 runs of at least 10 yards in five games.

"It's frustrating," Reagor said.

Informed he seemed unusually agitated considering the game's outcome, Reagor didn't dispute the observation.

"I am," he snapped. "I'm tired of people always asking me about it. We know it's a problem. We've just got to correct it. We don't want people to run on us."

Coach Tony Dungy shared Reagor's dissatisfaction but not his anger. He said the Colts initially had a problem with an option play the Titans ran with Young out of the shotgun formation.

"We didn't play it quite right," Dungy said, adding the defense eventually made the proper adjustments.

The defense also frequently overran plays, allowing Henry and White to do damage with cutbacks. Henry had one 14-yard run and three 17-yarders.

At halftime, the Titans had a 10-0 lead and the Colts' run defense had tire marks. Tennessee had rushed 21 times for 152 yards.

"It's unacceptable giving up 150 yards in the first half in a game, really," linebacker Gary Brackett said.

Once again, the defense found refuge in the locker room at halftime. It talked about what was going wrong, and adjusted.

"We settled down and played more relaxed," linebacker Cato June said.

Added Reagor: "Guys were better in their lanes and we flowed (to the ball) better."

The Titans were limited to 62 yards in the second half but still averaged a robust 6.2 yards per attempt. Credit the Colts' defense, but contributing was Tennessee's inability to convert third downs in the second half (1-for-5) and stay on the field.

For all its shortcomings, the defense made the requisite plays with the game on the line. The Titans managed only 86 yards in the final two quarters after piling up 191 in the first half.

After Peyton Manning gave the Colts their first lead at 14-13 with a 2-yard TD pass to Reggie Wayne with 5:10 remaining, the defense made it stand up.

"Obviously we're not happy giving up 152 (rushing) yards in the first half," June said. "That just can't happen. But we're 5-0. What's it matter if we give up 500 yards if we win?"

SMACKED, THEN SMOKIN'

Manning KOs Redskins with sizzling 3rd quarter

By Phil Richards

Peyton Manning left the field a few minutes before half-time Sunday at the RCA Dome for a quick medical check. He had been hit hard, and he came back like he was angry.

Manning hit 7-of-8 passes for 138 yards and three touchdowns during a white-hot third quarter that ignited a 36-22 Colts victory over the Washington Redskins.

"Real ugly," left guard Dylan Gandy said of a wicked double shot absorbed by Manning when he was hit low by Redskins end Andre Carter and high by defensive lineman Phillip Daniels.

Manning was bent backward and twisted sharply. His helmet was knocked off and his head slammed into the turf with such force that bits of granulized rubber from the FieldTurf embedded in his forehead.

◀ **ROUGHED UP:** Peyton Manning gets up off the turf after being sandwiched by the Redskins' Phillip Daniels and Andre Carter in the second quarter of the game.
Sam Riche / The Star

▶ **THAT'S RIGHT:** Colts new defensive tackle Anthony McFarland (92) pumps his fist after assisting on a tackle in the first quarter at the RCA Dome. Matt Kryger / The Star

NFL Week Seven

Colts 36
Redskins 22

Team record: 6-0

"You could feel it in the crowd, like everybody goes, 'Ohhhhhh,' because it's Peyton," said Colts tight end Ben Utecht. "For him to get up and stand in the pocket like that after a hit like that takes a lot of guts."

Manning finished with 25 completions in 35 pass attempts for 342 yards and four touchdowns as the Colts (6-0) won for the 18th time in their past 20 home games. His 14th four-touchdown game moved him to fourth on the NFL career list behind some extraordinarily distinguished names: Dan Marino (21), Bart Starr (19) and John Unitas (17).

Manning had nothing to say of the big hit or of another scary moment, when Redskins linebacker Marcus Washington dove or fell into him, bent him over backward and put Manning in the kind of position that can blow out a knee.

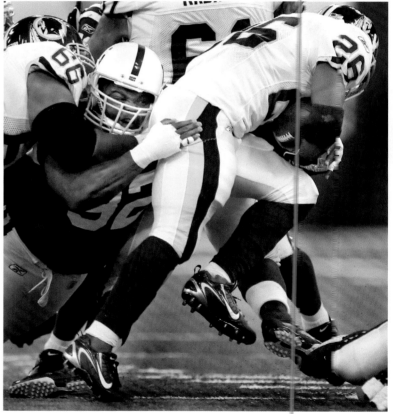

▲ **BIG IMPACT:** The Colts' new acquisition Anthony McFarland (92) takes down Redskins running back Clinton Portis (26) in first-half action. Sam Riche / The Star

◄ **SURVEYING THE FIELD:** Peyton Manning drops back to pass in the first quarter. Matt Kryger / The Star

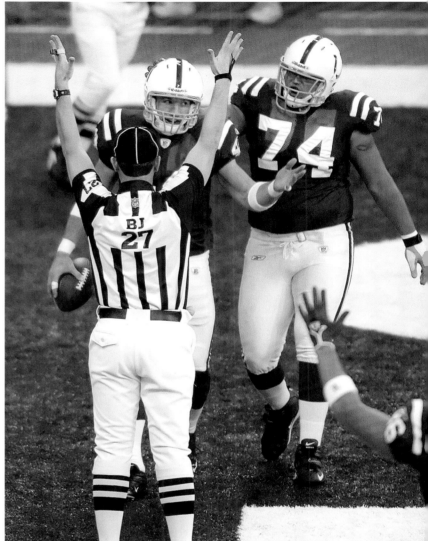

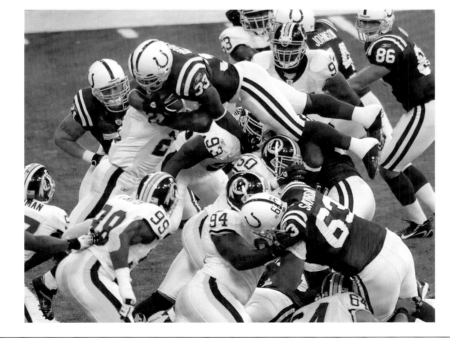

▲ **TRUE COLORS:** Colts fan Billy Slavens, Indianapolis, shows off his Colts colors at the RCA Dome. **Matt Kryger** / The Star

▲ **TOUCHDOWN!:** Colts tight end Dallas Clark celebrates his touchdown with Charlie Johnson (74) in the first quarter. **Matt Kryger** / The Star

◄ **STOPPED SHORT:** Colts running back Dominic Rhodes (33) attempts to dive over the Redskins line but fails to score a touchdown in the first quarter. **Matt Kryger** / The Star

"I attended the Bill Belichick school of not discussing injuries a few summers ago," Manning volunteered, and that was that. He didn't budge. He wouldn't discuss either hit nor the headache or sore neck he might or might not have had.

"He acted like he was hurt," said right guard Jake Scott, "but he's a tough guy. His consecutive starts streak shows that."

Manning has started the first 134 games of his career, an NFL record for quarterbacks.

Colts coach Tony Dungy said Manning left the field early so a team physician could give him a quick look.

While Manning wouldn't admit to being hurt, he did confess to being a little perturbed. A chal-

◀ **CHOKE HOLD:** Colts quarterback Peyton Manning is bent backwards by the Redskins' Phillip Daniels (93) and Andre Carter (99) in the second quarter.
Matt Detrich / The Star

▼ **KEEPING HIS HEAD:** Peyton Manning loses his helmet on the play.
Sam Riche / The Star

▲ **NICE GRAB:** Dallas Clark hauls in a pass from Peyton Manning in the first quarter. **Sam Riche** / The Star

lenge of his 1-yard touchdown pass to wide receiver Marvin Harrison during the final minute of the half was overturned after a video review.

"Kind of frustrating," Manning said.

Not during the third quarter.

With Manning throwing strikes and rookie running back Joseph Addai slashing through cracks and breaking tackles, the Colts went off like a rocket. Suddenly it was 33-14.

Manning hit wide receiver Marvin Harrison with touchdown passes of 4 yards and 1 yard. He connected with wide re-

◀**FANCY FOOTWORK:** Marvin Harrison (88) gets his feet down for a third-quarter touchdown in front of Redskins defensive back Shawn Springs. **Sam Riche** / The Star

◀**NO STOPPING HIM:** Reggie Wayne pulls in a pass from Peyton Manning and heads for the end zone in the third quarter. **Sam Riche** / The Star

▲ **WHO'S THE MAN?:** The Colts Reggie Wayne celebrates his 51-yard touchdown catch. **Robert Scheer** / The Star

ceiver Reggie Wayne on a 51-yarder. The latter couldn't have been more perfect had Manning been dropping a dime in a bucket.

Wayne finished with seven catches for 122 yards, Harrison with seven for 73 yards. Tight end Dallas Clark had the other touchdown reception, a 1-yarder.

If Manning was sore, he showed no signs. Of course he wouldn't. He never has.

"You get hit hard out there. It's a tough game," Dungy said. "I've seen him take some shots. He's a little tougher than people give him credit for. We don't like to find out how tough he is, but he's been hit in the five years I've been here."

Pretty numbers don't necessarily mean pretty quarterback. ■

▶ HELD DOWN: Colts wide receiver Reggie Wayne draws a pass interference penalty from Washington's Kenny Wright on a two-point conversion attempt in the third quarter. **Matt Detrich** / The Star

▼ SACK CELEBRATION: The Colts' Josh Thomas (91) reacts after sacking Redskins quarterback Mark Brunell in second-half action. **Sam Riche** / The Star

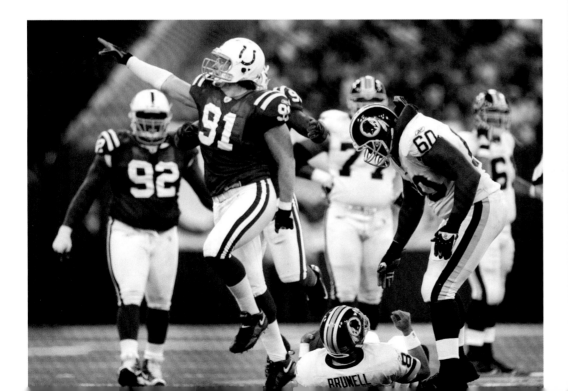

▲ **BREAKUP DANCE:** Colts defensive back Nick Harper reacts after breaking up a pass in the second half.
Sam Riche / The Star

◀ **CONGRATULATIONS:** Colts place-kicker Adam Vinatieri (4) is congratulated after hitting a 47-yard field goal. **Sam Riche** / The Star

◀◀ **THE WAVE:** Colts fans do 'the wave' during the third quarter.
Robert Scheer / The Star

▲ **SAD ENDING:** Washington fans had nothing to cheer about in the final minutes as they watched the Colts beat the Redskins 36-22. **Matt Detrich** / The Star

▶ **WELL-DESERVED REST:** Colts defenders Raheem Brock (79) and Dwight Freeney take a knee and watch the final seconds of the game tick away. **Sam Riche** / The Star

▼ **I'M FINE:** Peyton Manning heads off the field after the game. **Sam Riche** / The Star

BOB KRAVITZ'S REPORT CARD

B RUN OFFENSE: Dominic, bench. Bench, Dominic. Seriously, if it's not apparent by now that Joseph Addai is a special player who needs to run and catch the ball a whole lot more often than Dom Rhodes, then we're all watching a completely different game. The moment Addai began gashing Washington's run defense in the third quarter, it set up the play-action and made everything go — the way it used to with Edgerrin James. One complaint, though: They still don't run well in the red zone.

A− PASS OFFENSE: It wasn't just the numbers, although those were pretty remarkable. Most important, the Colts came out aggressively, even with Washington sitting back in that two-deep zone. For whatever reason, this passing game needs to get into an early rhythm, regardless of what the defense is giving. Huge games for Reggie Wayne and Marvin Harrison, and it was nice to see the tight ends getting involved once again.

B RUN DEFENSE: Hey, anything short of 150 yards, that's a great day. Maybe coach Tony Dungy should rip his defense as being "soft" every week. There was nothing soft and cuddly about this group this week, especially in the second half. Anthony "Booger" McFarland announced his presence on the first drive. Cato June seemed to be everywhere, although I won't know for sure until I look at the tape.

B PASS DEFENSE: OK, so this doesn't have much to do with the pass defense, but if I'm a Washington columnist, I'm wondering out loud what exactly the Redskins are trying to accomplish. The old Joe Gibbs 'Skins were a power running team. Now, they're all about draws and screens, dink passes and 700-page playbooks. And you wonder, do they get paid by the dumb penalty? At the prices owner Dan Snyder pays, the Redskins ought to be a whole lot better, and more disciplined.

D+ SPECIAL TEAMS: OK, so they were terrific in the second half. The Terrence Wilkins kick return got the third quarter moving in the right direction. The kick coverage was excellent in the second half. And Adam Vinatieri overcame the fact his own team iced him with a goofy timeout. But if I'm Russ Purnell, the special teams coach, I'm looking over my shoulder. Except for Week 1, special teams has made a blunder every game that nearly doomed this team. (In an unrelated note, explain to me how Antwaan Randle El's celebration could be deemed excessive.) Got to say, I enjoyed watching Washington kick off from the 5-yard line. Just when you thought you'd seen it all . . .

B COACHING: Give them credit for improvising on the run. How often do you show up at the stadium on Sunday and find out one of your top defensive linemen is in the hospital after a car wreck? Pretty good timing, bringing in McFarland this week. Dungy isn't a fire-and-brimstone guy at halftime — he doesn't do fire or brimstone — but his calm, matter-of-fact approach has been perfect for this team. All year, they've come alive in the second half.

B INTANGIBLES: I am terribly sad to report that Hunter Smith, Vice President in Charge of Intangibles, has resigned his post, effective immediately. Apparently, he has an out clause in his contract that allows him to fulfill his lifelong dream of doing intangibles for the Terre Haute Tribune-Star. In the meantime, I'm accepting applications and resumes. Corey Simon is not eligible for the position.

W, AS IN WAYNE

Receiver catches 3 second-half touchdowns

By Phil Richards

DENVER — A Denver defense that had yielded 44 points to its first six opponents gave up 34 Sunday. A Denver defense that hadn't given up a touchdown in 14 quarters at Invesco Field at Mile High gave up three during the second half Sunday.

Reggie Wayne scored all of them. He was in his element.

"It's like a playoff atmosphere," Wayne bubbled after the Indianapolis Colts' 34-31 victory over the Denver Broncos. "You know it's going to be a hostile crowd. You've gotta love playing here, the 75,000 go to cheering and the stadium goes to shaking and it gives you goose bumps.

"Those are the times you want to step up and make plays. My number was called today."

Quarterback Peyton Manning did the calling. Manning completed 32-of-39 passes for 345 yards and three touchdowns. Ten of

NFL Week Eight

Colts 34
Broncos 31

Team record: 7-0

◄**GOT IT:** Colts wide receiver Reggie Wayne catches a touchdown pass with 3:35 left as Denver's Darrent Williams tries to defend. It was Wayne's third touchdown. **Matt Detrich** / The Star

▶**THIRD TIME'S A CHARM:** Reggie Wayne is lifted into the air by teammate Dallas Clark as he celebrates his third touchdown of the game along with Jeff Saturday. That score and a two-point conversion put the Colts ahead 31-28. **Matt Detrich** / The Star

those passes and all of those touchdowns went to Wayne, who accounted for 138 yards.

"He called it before the game," Colts defensive end Dwight Freeney reported. "Reggie said, 'I'm going to kill the Broncos.'"

Denver's NFL-best 13-game home winning streak died with it. The Broncos (5-2) played 58 noble minutes of hard-hitting football. They achieved a 31-31 stalemate on Jason Elam's 49-yard field goal with 1:49 to play. Too much time.

The Colts (7-0) grabbed a two-game lead and the head-to-head tiebreaker on Denver in the chase for the AFC's No. 1 playoff seed. The visitors maintained their AFC South lead at three games over Jacksonville and became the first team to start consecutive seasons 7-0 since the 1929-31 Green Bay Packers. No other team has done it twice.

Manning completed all five of his pass attempts for 47 yards — two to Wayne for 22 yards — while engineering his third fourth-quarter game-winning drive in the Colts' last four games. Adam Vinatieri drove the football through the uprights for the fourth time in as many tries, this time from 37 yards with the clock reading 0:02.

▲ **WAITING AND HOPING:** C.C. Burrup, 8, Pocatello, Idaho, waits for Colts players to pass as he hopes for an autograph inside Invesco Field at Mile High. **Robert Scheer** / The Star

▶ **TAKING TIME TO SIGN:** Dwight Freeney signs some autographs prior to kickoff. **Robert Scheer**/ The Star

▲ **PUMPKIN HEAD:** A Broncos fan dressed as a scarecrow and holding a Colts horse on a noose entertains the crowd. **Matt Detrich** / The Star

▼ **SAY WHAT?:** Colts defensive back Dexter Reid taunts the Denver crowd as they give him a hard time before the start of the game. **Matt Detrich**/ The Star

▲ **FLAGGED:** Reggie Wayne (87) can't quite get to this ball as he is defended by Darrent Williams (left) and John Lynch. Wayne was called for offensive pass interference on this first-quarter play. **Robert Scheer** / The Star

◀ **BREAKAWAY:** Colts running back Dominic Rhodes breaks away against a Denver defender in the first quarter. **Matt Detrich**/ The Star

It was great drama.

The defense played tough for a half, then got run over. Denver rushed 36 times for 227 yards and three touchdowns. The Colts offense rendered it all meaningless. Three times during the fourth quarter it came from behind to take the lead.

"It's such an honor to play on an offense like this," left tackle Tarik

▲ **NO WAY:** Gary Brackett of the Colts (left) raises his hands in protest as he is flagged for roughing Broncos quarterback Jake Plummer, background, on this first-quarter play. Robert Scheer / The Star

▶ **HARD STOP:** Colts defensive lineman Anthony McFarland puts a stop to Denver running back Tatum Bell in the second quarter. Matt Detrich / The Star

Glenn said. "You look around the huddle and you could see it in Reggie's and Marvin Harrison's eyes. You could see it in Dallas (Clark's) and the other tight ends. All the offensive line knew. It's a trust factor."

Too much self-assurance. Too many weapons. Too much time.

While six-time Pro Bowl cornerback Champ Bailey was getting help covering seven-time Pro Bowl wide receiver Harrison, Manning was checking down, finding Wayne and Clark and running back Joseph Addai, who rushed 17 times for 93 yards.

▲ **AUDIBLE OFFENSE:** Peyton Manning (18) calls an audible during second-quarter action. **Robert Scheer** / The Star

◄ **FLIPPED:** Denver running back Mike Bell is flipped in the air by the Colts defense as he attempts to get into the end zone from the 3-yard line. Bell was stopped on the 1-yard line, but the Broncos scored on the possession in the second quarter. **Matt Detrich** / The Star

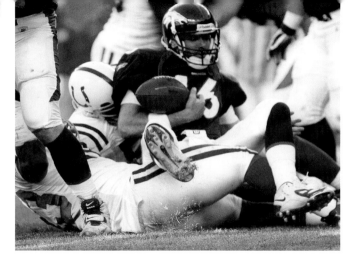

◀◀ NICE DAY FOR ADDAI: Colts running back Joseph Addai (29) takes a handoff from Peyton Manning. Addai totaled 93 rushing yards on 17 attempts. Robert Scheer / The Star

◀ SHAKE IT LOOSE: The ball comes loose as Denver quarterback Jake Plummer is pulled down by Colts defenders. Plummer was ruled down by officials on the field, but after a video review, the play was ruled a fumble that the Colts recovered. Robert Scheer / The Star

▼ WAYNE SCORES ... AGAIN: Reggie Wayne hauls in this third-quarter touchdown against the defense of Darrent Williams (left) and Nick Ferguson of the Broncos. Robert Scheer / The Star

Like Wayne, Manning was in his element. He loved the crowd of 76,767, third-largest in Broncos history. He loved the competition with the worthy Broncos. He loved the pressure. He loved the fourth quarter.

"When you're back and forth and know it's going to be a four-quarter game, I'm enjoying it," Manning said. "I'm enjoying playing."

Often as not, while Manning was going through his checks, Wayne was drawing single

KRAVITZ ON THE COLTS

The Indianapolis Colts' offense dressed on one side of the visitors' locker room at Invesco Field at Mile High. The Colts' defense dressed on the other side. On the offensive side, there were smiles, lots of happy chatter. On the defensive side, where the boys were either breathless or sickened or a little bit of both, there was mostly silence.

At the risk of dropping a damp rag on what's been another amazing 7-0 start — the only other team to do that twice in a row was the 1929-31 Green Bay Packers, who did it three straight years — it has to be mentioned now, as the cheers die down and the stars fade from our eyes: If this Indianapolis run defense doesn't get better, much better, we're looking at another season without a championship.

coverage. He destroyed Broncos cornerback Darrent Williams. Again and again and again.

Wayne slashed inside Williams on a quick post route for his first touchdown, a 12-yarder during the third quarter. He ran past him again three minutes later to score on a 5-yard reception.

Then, with the Colts facing third-and-2 from the Denver 19, Wayne lulled Williams, Manning pump-faked and Wayne took off to catch the touchdown pass that made it 29-28. Of course, Manning went back to Wayne on the successful two-point conversion.

"I'm not going to apologize," Wayne said. "I'm going to work just like he's going to work. When I'm out there, I just refuse to lose."

That's what this game was all about. The Colts refused to lose. ■

▲ **FOCUS:** Tony Dungy on the sideline. **Robert Scheer** / The Star

▶ **TOUCHDOWN!:** Reggie Wayne celebrates after one of his two third-quarter touchdowns against the Broncos. **Robert Scheer** / The Star

◄◄ **ADDAI STOPPED:** Colts running back Joseph Addai is brought down by Denver's Jerome Collins in the closing minute of the game. Matt Detrich / The Star

◄ **IT'S GOOD!:** Colts kicker Adam Vinatieri boots the game-winning field goal with two seconds left. Matt Detrich / The Star

▼ **PEEK-A-BOO:** Vinatieri, who is no stranger to game-winning field goals, looks through a scrum of Colts players congratulating him for his 37-yard field goal.

Robert Scheer / The Star

▶ **HE DID IT AGAIN:** Manning is the center of attention as he heads to the locker room after marching the team into position for a game-winning field goal. He got the ball at his 20 with 1:49 left and moved the team to Denver's 18.
Matt Detrich / The Star

▼ **CELEBRATION:** Colts center Jeff Saturday (left) and offensive tackle Tarik Glenn celebrate as they head for the locker room. **Matt Detrich** / The Star

▲ **A GOOD DAY'S WORK:** Reggie Wayne of the Colts comes off the field after the game. **Robert Scheer** / The Star

Manning delivers another comeback

By Mike Chappell

DENVER — Another dramatic ending — what is it, five, six this season? — was ushered in by an idyllic beginning.

During pregame warm-ups Sunday at Invesco Field at Mile High, Indianapolis Colts quarterback Peyton Manning paused from his meticulous preparation to drink in the atmosphere created by a mix of a sellout crowd of 76,767 and the 70-degree temperature.

He saw the crowd, felt it in his bones.

"What a great atmosphere out there," he said. "That makes you want to have an outdoor stadium.

"You're focusing on your timing and getting ready. But I told (position coach) Jim Caldwell, 'This is a heck of a day for football.' Reminded me of Saturdays back in Knoxville (Tenn.). Great crowd and they've got a great team."

Just not great enough. Not Sunday. Not against the Colts as long as the Manning-led offense had enough time — just one more possession — to put a perfect ending on a perfect afternoon.

Colts 34, Broncos 31.

For the third time this season and 26th time in his nine-year career, Manning directed the Colts on a fourth-quarter game-winning drive. This time, it was through the heart of a Denver defense that entered the game ranked No. 1 in the NFL in points allowed but exited with only praise for Manning and his supporting cast.

"Even if you play well against them in the beginning, you still have to bring it for 60 minutes," Denver safety John Lynch said.

The Colts trailed 14-6 at the half as the Broncos limited Indy's self-destructing offense to a pair of Adam Vinatieri field goals. In the second half, Denver

had no answers. Consider the Colts' second-half productivity: three Manning-to-Reggie Wayne touchdown passes, two more Vinatieri field goals, including the game-winning 37-yarder with two seconds remaining, 260 total yards.

Manning, once again, was the maestro. In the second half he completed 18-of-22 passes for 213 yards and the three TDs.

"When you make a mistake," Lynch said, "he will expose it."

Coach Tony Dungy appeared unmoved by Manning's latest theatrics. That, Dungy seemed to insinuate, is what you expect from a two-time NFL Most Valuable Player.

"You can't overemphasize how good the quarterback is," he said. "People try to do different things and he just follows his reads and throws to the right guy."

Most of the time Sunday that was Wayne. He had 10 receptions for 138 yards, routinely victimizing Denver cornerback Darrent Williams. But this was not an afternoon of simple pitch-and-catch between Manning and Wayne. Six other Colts caught at least one pass.

And there's no understating the impact of rookie running back Joseph Addai. He had the best game of his young career, carrying 17 times for 93 yards and catching five passes for 37 yards.

Three times in the second half the Colts had to come back from deficits or a tie. Three times they executed, prevailed.

After directing the Colts to a 31-28 lead with 3:35

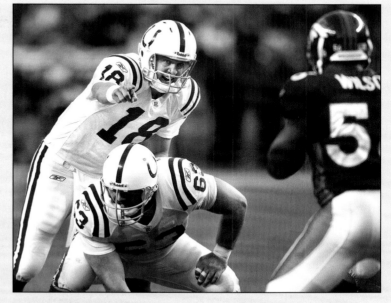

▲ HERE'S THE PLAN: Peyton Manning calls an audible at the line of scrimmage. The crowd in Denver was so loud, it made it hard to hear at times in the fourth quarter. Matt Detrich/ The Star

remaining with his 19-yard touchdown to Wayne, Manning was forced to reload when Jason Elam's 49-yard field goal produced a 31-31 stalemate.

But 1 minute, 49 seconds remained. A lifetime for Manning.

He went 5-for-5 for 47 yards on the final drive. After an early 5-yard run, Addai took a draw 9 yards to the Denver 18.

Seconds remained. In came Vinatieri. Game over.

"It would have been nice to stop them and not have to have those two drives," Dungy said. "But when our offense has the ball with a chance to win, we feel pretty good about it."

PRIMETIME PUNCHOUT

5 takeaways help Indy remain only unbeaten

By **Phil Richards**

FOXBOROUGH, Mass. — Peyton Manning piled up the big numbers but the Indianapolis Colts' much-maligned defense made a bunch of the big plays as it contributed five takeaways to the Colts' 27-20 victory over the New England Patriots at rowdy, chilly Gillette Stadium.

It's only midseason, but the Colts' 30th victory in their past 33 regular-season games pushed them to 8-0 and gave them what amounts to a three-game lead on the Patriots (6-2) in the chase for the AFC's No. 1 playoff seed, because of the head-to-head tiebreaker. The Colts are at least two games ahead of everyone else in the conference and remained three up on Jacksonville (5-3) in the AFC South.

◀ALL LINED UP: Colts coach Tony Dungy is all smiles as he celebrates the win with center Jeff Saturday (left) and offensive tackle Tarik Glenn after their 27-20 win against the Patriots. **Matt Detrich** / The Star

▶ DELIVERING THE BLOW: Dwight Freeney hits Patriots quarterback Tom Brady (12) in the fourth quarter. **Matt Kryger** / The Star

NFL Week Nine

Colts 27
Patriots 20

Team record: 8-0

It was the Colts' second consecutive victory at New England after a run of nine losses in succession here.

Manning completed 20-of-36 passes for 326 yards and two touchdowns to become only the second Colts quarterback to throw for 300 yards in three consecutive games. John Unitas did it in 1963.

"You have to win as a team," Manning told an NBC reporter after the game. "You can't win playing as an individual against these guys."

The Colts embodied team. On a night when they were outrushed 148 yards to 53, the defense kept taking the football away.

▶ **NO CHOKING HERE:** Patriots fans had no idea of what was to come as Peyton Manning and the Colts did not choke and went on to a 27-20 win against the New England Patriots. **Matt Detrich** / The Star

▶▶ **GOOD START:** The Colts' Antoine Bethea (41) intercepts a Tom Brady pass in the first quarter. **Matt Detrich** / The Star

▲ **BAD HAIR DAY?:** Colts fans (from the left) Ed Herman, Carmel, Ind., Bradley Herman, Randy Ragin and Situ Mistry cheer on the Colts. **Matt Kryger** / The Star

▶ **SIGN OF SUPPORT:** A Colts fan cheers for her team before the start of the game. **Matt Kryger** / The Star

Defensive tackle Raheem Brock forced and recovered a fumble. Safety Antoine Bethea intercepted one pass in the Colts end zone. Safety Bob Sanders stole another at the Colts 3-yard line.

The second of linebacker Cato June's pair of interceptions came on a pass that deflected off Patriots running back Kevin Faulk and put the game away. It came with 1:18 to play with New England driving and at the Colts 39.

"They were around the ball," Patriots quarterback Tom Brady said. "They've got good aggressiveness on defense. They got their hands on it. They didn't drop any."

▶ **IN TRAFFIC:** Marvin Harrison (88) makes a catch in front of the Patriots' Rodney Harrison (far right) and Colts tight end Dallas Clark (44) in the first quarter. Matt Kryger / The Star

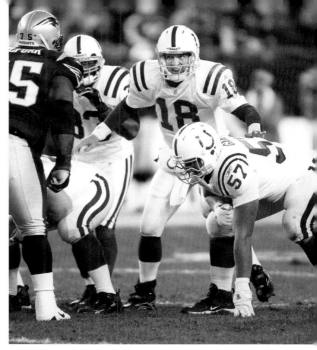

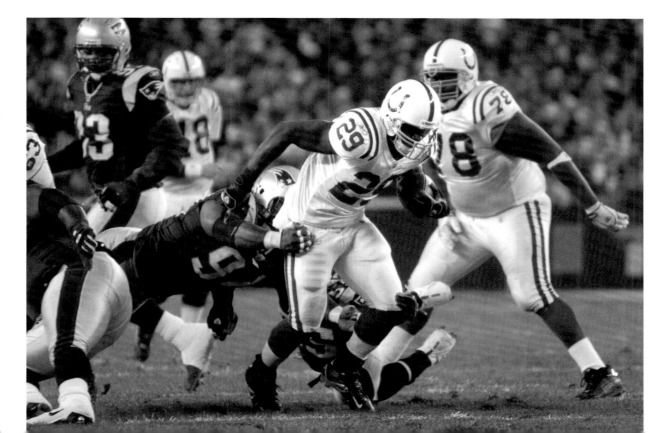

▲ **ANOTHER CATCH FOR HARRISON:** Marvin Harrison (88) makes a catch in front of the Patriots' Chad Clark in the first quarter. **Matt Kryger** / The Star

▲ **ADJUSTMENTS:** Colts quarterback Peyton Manning (18) changes the play at the line in the first quarter.
Matt Detrich / The Star

◄ **CAN'T CATCH HIM:** Joseph Addai (29) outruns the tackle of Marquise Hill in the first quarter.
Matt Kryger / The Star

Adam Vinatieri, who played the first 10 years of his career for New England before signing with the Colts as a free agent in the offseason, had a forgettable homecoming night. He converted 23- and 31-yard field goals but missed from 37 and 46. He was booed throughout by the sellout crowd of 68,756.

Colts wide receiver Marvin Harrison caught eight passes for 145 yards and two touchdowns. It was his seventh 100-yard game against the Patriots, two more than he has against any other NFL team.

Harrison's most spectacular catch was for the third-quarter game-winner,

▶**EYES ON THE PRIZE:** Colts wide receiver Marvin Harrison keeps his concentration on the ball as he splits Patriots' defenders Mike Vrabel (50) and Ellis Hobbs (27) to make this third-quarter catch. **Matt Detrich** / The Star

▼**TOES DOWN:** Harrison keeps his focus as he drags his toes to stay in the end zone for a touchdown. The play gave the Colts a 24-14 lead in the third quarter. **Matt Detrich** / The Star

▲ **GOOD COVER:** Reggie Wayne (87) fails to catch a pass in the end zone as the Patriots' Asante Samuel defends in the second quarter. **Matt Kryger** / The Star

the touchdown that gave the Colts a 24-14 lead. He beat cornerback Ellis Hobbs into the end zone. Harrison stretched with his left hand, tipped Manning's pass, then gathered it in and got both feet down before he fell out of bounds.

It was touch, artistry, ballet. And it came against one of the NFL's top defenses.

New England hadn't permitted a touchdown in its past two games and was the only team in the league that hadn't allowed an opponent

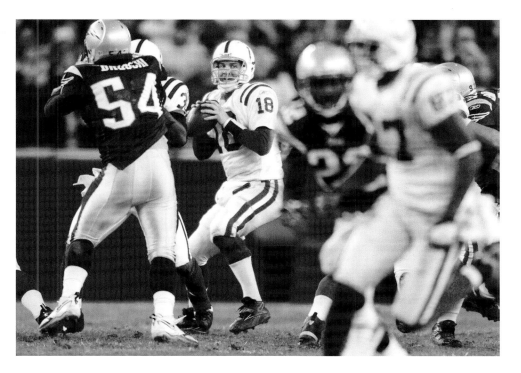

▲ **FINDING WAYNE:** Peyton Manning (18) drops back to pass to Reggie Wayne (right) in the third quarter.

Matt Kryger / The Star

▶ **END-ZONE CELEBRATION:** Raheem Brock (79) flies into the air to bump with teammate Cato June after Brock picked up a fumble and ran to the end zone in the third quarter. After a review, the play was ruled a fumble recovery but brought back to the 30-yard line. **Matt Detrich** / The Star

to score more than 17 points in a game all season.

"The thing I like about our team is we're finding different ways to win," Colts coach Tony Dungy said. "We're still not playing our best."

Manning came into the game on a roll. In victories over Washington and Denver, he had thrown for 342 yards and four touchdowns and 345 yards and three touchdowns, respectively.

After missing his first two passes Sunday, he hit his next nine for 140 yards and two touchdowns as the Colts took a 14-7 lead.

"We had them in a chase position most of the night," Manning said. "That was part of the plan and it worked out well for us." ■

KRAVITZ ON THE COLTS

So how's that for a road trip? Go to Denver, the toughest place in the NFL to win a game, and treat the league's best defense with utter contempt.

Then come to New England, home of the game's most recent dynasty, and not only beat the Patriots 27-20, but do so without playing anything close to your best game.

You know what this means now, don't you? The Perfect Season talk can begin. The magic number talk can begin. And the debate over whether coach Tony Dungy should rest his starters after the Indianapolis Colts have sewn up home-field advantage can begin.

Eight-and-oh.

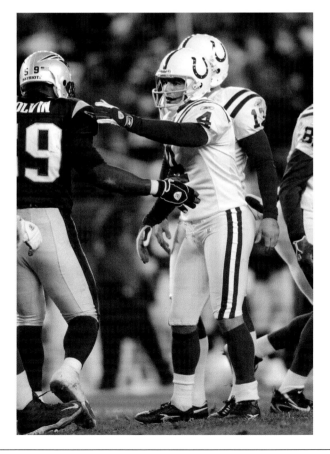

▲ **AVOIDING THE SACK:** Peyton Manning gets the ball away just before getting hit by the Patriots' Jarvis Green (97) in the fourth quarter. **Matt Kryger** / The Star

◄ **DIFFERENT SIDES:** Colts kicker Adam Vinatieri (4) gives former Patriots teammate Rosevelt Colvin a pat after Vinatieri made a field goal in the fourth quarter. **Matt Kryger** / The Star

Brady suffers through rough night

By Phillip B. Wilson

FOXBOROUGH, Mass. — The roles were reversed for a second consecutive November.

The champion blinked. The unbeaten underdog did not.

Once upon a playoff time, Indianapolis made the mistakes and couldn't handle New England's pressure. Now, it's the Patriots' Tom Brady throwing more interceptions than the Colts' Peyton Manning, and the Colts departing Gillette Stadium on Sunday with a 27-20 victory.

Brady threw four interceptions. The Patriots also lost a fumble.

The Colts, who won here 40-21 to go to 8-0 last year, took advantage of their hosts' generosity to stay perfect again after eight games. Different year, same claim. Indy exited as the AFC's team to beat. New England, a three-time Super Bowl champion since 2001, has to play catch-up in the second half of the season.

"It was a tough night all the way around," said Brady, who fell to 0-7 in games in which he has three or more interceptions. "Obviously, we need to play better than that.

"We were playing a good team. The defense really kept us in there with as many turnovers as there were. You can't really expect to win when you play the way we played."

Counting the playoffs, the Patriots had Manning's number until last year. They beat him his first seven trips here. The two-time league MVP had been humbled in frigid back-to-back playoff losses.

Brady, who won his first six starts against Manning, is the more celebrated winner. He is a two-time Super Bowl MVP. He has three rings. Manning

has none.

But Brady's first interception was on an ill-advised deep ball on the opening possession. Colts rookie safety Antoine Bethea just drifted over and caught it in the end zone.

"It was just one of those nights," Brady said.

The Patriots' leader had a similar deep ball picked off by safety Bob Sanders at the end of the first half.

The other two interceptions were not Brady's fault. Colts linebacker Cato June grabbed both. The first was tipped at the line by the Colts' Robert Mathis. The second went right through the hands of Patriots running back Kevin Faulk. It snuffed out the Patriots' last gasp in the closing minutes.

Patriots coach Bill Belichick blamed himself.

"I didn't do a good enough job of coaching. We didn't do a good enough job of playing," he said.

The Colts had two turnovers. Manning was intercepted once. His 36 passes were one more than Brady, and both completed 20. But Manning passed for 326 yards; Brady had just 201.

The Patriots had committed eight turnovers in the previous seven games. The Colts had entered with just 11 takeaways, including five interceptions.

Belichick didn't wish to concern himself with playoff ramifications.

"Look, I don't care about that," he said. "The only thing we were concerned about was trying to win this game. The next week, we play the (New York) Jets.

▲ **GOING DOWN:** New England quarterback Tom Brady (12) is brought down by Colts linebacker Cato June in the third quarter. Matt Detrich / The Star

Wherever we finish, they will tell us what we're supposed to do.

"The rest of that stuff, you guys can worry about that."

The Patriots were supposed to have a decided edge against the Colts' league-worst run defense. And while they ran for 148 yards and averaged 4.5 per carry, it wasn't near enough to overcome the turnovers.

"We weren't consistently productive running the ball. We weren't consistently productive throwing it," Belichick said. "We just didn't play well enough to win."

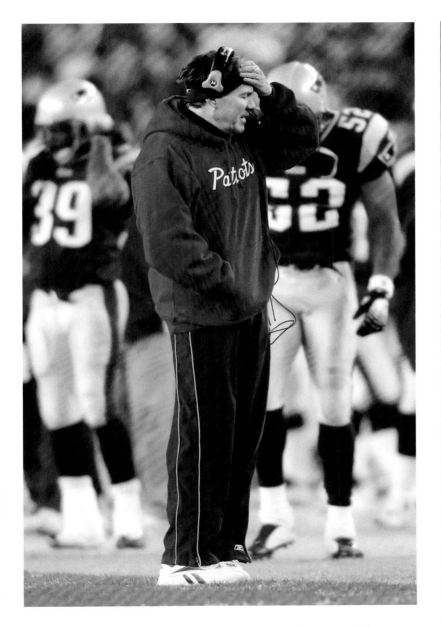

▲ **DISBELIEF:** New England coach Bill Belichick can't believe the outcome of the game. **Matt Kryger** / The Star

◀ **POSTGAME CELEBRATION:** Colts defensive back Antoine Bethea (41) celebrates the Colts' win with teammate Tyjuan Hagler as they head to the locker room after the 27-20 victory against the New England Patriots. **Matt Detrich** / The Star

Sanders back for Colts 'D'

By Mike Chappell

FOXBOROUGH, Mass. — The Indianapolis Colts defense received a pregame boost when Bob Sanders was activated for Sunday night's AFC showdown with the New England Patriots.

The team's Pro Bowl safety missed the previous five games after undergoing arthroscopic surgery on his right knee in September. However, Sanders went through a strenuous workout at Gillette Stadium approximately two hours before the game and did enough to convince the coaching staff he was ready to return to the lineup.

▲ **HE'S BACK:** Colts safety Bob Sanders (21) gets up after stopping Patriots running back Kevin Faulk in the fourth quarter. **Matt Kryger** / The Star

The Colts' run defense entered Sunday night's game as the NFL's worst, allowing 167.9 yards per game and 5.4 yards per attempt. While poor execution has contributed to the poor performance, there's no denying the impact injuries have had on the porous run defense.

Defensive tackle Corey Simon has not played this season and will miss the final eight games because of a knee injury and an undisclosed illness. And defensive tackle Montae Reagor missed his third straight game after fracturing his left orbital bone in an Oct. 22 car accident.

Sanders has been a 5-8, 206-pound enforcer for the defense. He started 14 games in 2005 and finished second on the team with 118 tackles. His 71 solo tackles also ranked second on the team.

While Sanders was out, Mike Doss and Marlin Jackson filled his spot in the starting lineup. Doss started four games before suffering a season-ending knee injury against Washington. Jackson, a cornerback, started last week at Denver.

TWO IN A ROW AT 9-0

Colts make NFL history by extending perfect start

By Phil Richards

On a day the Indianapolis Colts made history, their much demeaned defense stood tall.

This time, the Colts didn't take the hits, they made them. With the RCA Dome sell-out crowd of 57,306 shouting "Deeefense. Deeefense," the Colts permitted a season-low 162 net yards to beat Buffalo 17-16 and become the first team in the NFL's 87-year history to start consecutive seasons 9-0.

The defense wasn't much more impressed with the record than with itself.

"Something to tell my kids, I guess," said middle linebacker Rob Morris, who made eight tackles while filling in for injured starter Gary Brackett. "But really, the ultimate goal is to get the ring. That's what we're focused on."

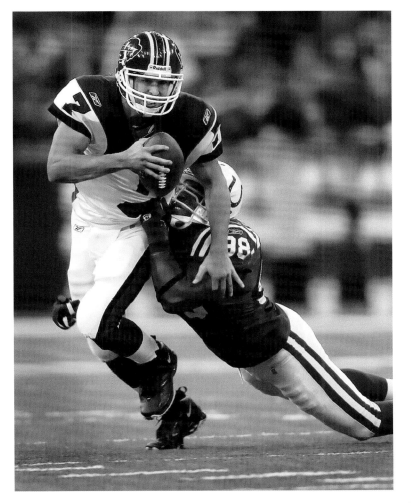

◄ADDAI FOR SIX: The Colts' Joseph Addai (29) runs for a 5-yard touchdown against the Buffalo Bills in the third quarter. Matt Kryger / The Star

▶STRETCHING THE MATERIAL: Colts defensive end Robert Mathis hangs on and sacks Bills quarterback JP Losman in the fourth quarter. The Colts totaled four sacks, including two by Mathis, in a 17-16 victory over Buffalo. Matt Kryger / The Star

NFL Week Ten

Colts 17
Bills 16

Team record: 9-0

On an afternoon the coverage teams struggled and the offense operated in fits and spurts, the defense dug in.

It yielded only three field goals. It kept Buffalo (3-5) out of the end zone. It permitted an average of 3.6 yards on 31 rushes, sacked quarterback JP Losman four times and limited him to 83 yards on 8-of-12 passing.

The Bills' lone touchdown came on cornerback Terrence McGee's 68-yard return of tight end Ben Utecht's fumble. McGee also set up a field goal with an 88-yard kickoff return.

The latter was one of several times the Colts defense was thrown into cri-

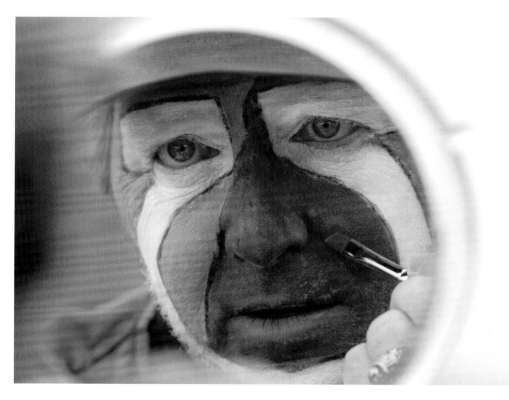

▲ **PUTTING ON HIS GAME FACE:** Colts fan Charles Howard, Indianapolis, applies the final touches of make-up as he gets ready for the game against the Buffalo Bills. **Matt Kryger** / The Star

▶ **KEEPING WARM:** Luke Taylor, 5, Zionsville, Ind., tries to stay warm while tailgating before the game.
Sam Riche / The Star

▲ **THIS JUST IN:** The Colts' Reggie Wayne (left) beats the Bills' Terrence McGee and deftly catches this pass for a touchdown during first-half action.
Sam Riche / The Star

▶ **GANG TACKLE:** Anthony Thomas of the Bills is wrapped up by Colts Anthony McFarland (left), Antoine Bethea (right) and Cato June. **Robert Scheer** / The Star

▼ **TAKE THAT:** June celebrates after stopping the Bills on a second-quarter play. June led Indy with nine tackles.
Matt Kryger / The Star

sis on a short field.

"We used to have a saying back at Michigan," said linebacker Cato June, a former Wolverines safety. " 'Just give me a place to stand. Wherever they spot the ball, we have to keep them out of the end zone.' "

The Colts did that after McGee's 88-yard return to the Indianapolis 12. Buffalo had to settle for Rian Lindell's 30-yard field goal. Four plays produced zero yards.

"We got stout when we had to," Morris said.

It happened again with the game on the line midway through the fourth quarter. Colts running back Dominic Rhodes fumbled, and Bills cornerback Nate Clements returned the football 8 yards to the Indianapolis 41.

The score was 17-16. The Bills marched sprightly to the Colts 17, where they faced third-and-5 with less than seven minutes to play.

Losman didn't have time to look downfield most of the day, yet Buffalo decided to block Pro Bowl defensive end Dwight Freeney with tight end Robert Royal. It was a classic mismatch. Freeney bulled past Royal and hammered Losman before the quarterback had time to set his feet.

"Big play. Big play in the game," June said. "That's what we expect from our front four, to get pressure and we can sit in our cover-2."

Losman went down hard for a 6-yard loss. Rather than a first down, or at least about a 35-yard field goal attempt, Lindell was kicking from 41 yards. His attempt sailed wide right.

The Colts consumed the final 6:22 with a 10-play drive, on which rookie running back Joseph Addai was the prime mover. Addai carried seven times for 41 yards.

Buffalo's offense has much about which to be modest. The Bills are not a quick-strike team. They have had trouble protecting

▲ **OOPS:** Colts tight end Ben Utecht (86) is stripped of the ball by Angelo Crowell. The fumble was returned for a Bills touchdown. **Sam Riche** / The Star

▲ **TOUGH GOING:** Colts running back Dominic Rhodes (left) runs into Buffalo's London Fletcher-Baker. **Matt Kryger** / The Star

▶**BRINGING HIM DOWN:** The Colts' Anthony McFarland sacks Bills quarterback JP Losman in first-half action. **Sam Riche** / The Star

Losman. They played without starting running back Willis McGahee, who suffered three broken ribs last week against Green Bay.

But Buffalo makes its living running the ball and backup Anthony Thomas is a competent 222-pound slammer. Thomas ran 28 times for 109 yards, a 3.9-yard average, against the league's worst rushing defense.

With safety Bob Sanders out, the Colts moved rookie Antoine Bethea from free safety down into the box at strong safety, and put cornerback Marlin Jackson at free safety. Bethea responded with eight tackles.

Everyone attacked.

"We knew they were going to come in and try to pound the ball, but everybody made their tackles," said cornerback Nick Harper, who was credited with six. "We didn't have too many missed tackles today and that was huge. People weren't diving at legs; everybody was hitting people in the chest where they needed to."

Good teams, Colts coach Tony Dungy told his players, find ways to win. On Sunday it was the defense's turn.

After giving up a 60-yard drive on Buffalo's opening possession, the Colts gave up 19 yards and a single first down on the Bills' next four series.

Deeefense, deeefense, indeed. ■

▲ **IMITATING THE QB:** Colts fan Sherman L. Whitfield, Zionsville, Ind., does his impersonation of Peyton Manning in the Colts quarterback's cell phone commercial. Sam Riche / The Star

◀ **END-ZONE ECSTASY:** Joseph Addai celebrates his 5-yard touchdown run agianst the Bills in the third quarter. Matt Kryger / The Star

KRAVITZ ON THE COLTS

Pardon the "any given Sunday" cliche-mongering, but it's only a cliche because it's true. And it makes the Colts' second straight 9-0 start — a historic first that won't soon be duplicated in the salary-cap era — all the more remarkable.

You think Curly Lambeau, the architect of those 1929, '30 and '31 Green Bay Packers teams, had to worry about losing his running back and best linebacker because of salary considerations?

Other elite NFL teams have their sub-standard performances and lose, like the Patriots and Falcons and Vikings and Jaguars and, well, you get the idea.

The Colts? They commit turnovers (rare) and stink out the joint on kick coverage (not so rare), and they win. They just win. Week after week after incredible week. Forget style points, or asterisks: * yeah, but they barely beat Jacksonville, the Jets, Tennessee and Buffalo. The Colts won most of last year's regular-season games in an elegant and often overwhelming style, and what exactly did that get them?

I can promise you, in locales such as New England and Kansas City and Atlanta, they're not gnashing their teeth about a lack of style. In those cities, full-scale panic has set in.

▲ **FIRST SACK:** Dwight Freeney (left) sacks Bills quarterback JP Losman in the fourth quarter. **Matt Kryger** / The Star

▶**FINALLY!:** Dwight Freeney (93) of the Colts celebrates this fourth-quarter sack of JP Losman. It was Freeney's first full sack of the year. **Robert Scheer** / The Star

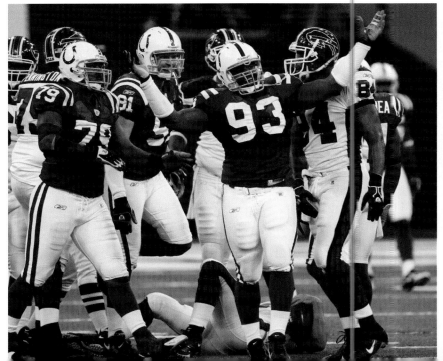

A pretty, ugly game

By Mike Chappell

In the end Sunday afternoon at the RCA Dome, everything was perfect for the Indianapolis Colts.

Quarterback Peyton Manning directed a methodical, clock-consuming 10-play drive.

Rookie running back Joseph Addai did the heavy lifting, carrying six times for 39 yards. Half of his attempts generated first downs.

And the Colts remained the NFL's only unbeaten and became the only team in league history to open consecutive seasons 9-0 with a 17-16 victory over the Buffalo Bills.

Purrr-fect.

"It was a good win," said Manning, who passed for 236 yards and a 1-yard touchdown to Reggie Wayne.

The Colts' collective perfection, though, was achieved on an otherwise error-filled afternoon. It wouldn't be a stretch to say they won in spite of themselves. Consider:

- Tight end Ben Utecht's second-quarter fumble after a 9-yard reception with the Colts leading 10-3 and driving for more. Bills cornerback Terrence McGee scooped it up and returned it, untouched, 68 yards for a touchdown.
- Running back Dominic Rhodes' lost fumble at the Colts 41-yard line midway through the fourth quarter. It gave the Bills a short field, which they promptly squandered when Rian Lindell pushed a 41-yard field goal attempt wide right.

- Four offensive penalties, two of which helped stall second-half drives.

Coach Tony Dungy was especially dissatisfied with the carelessness of what had been a productive and protective offense. The Colts entered the game with just six turnovers, tied for fewest in the league.

"I thought we'd be a little sharper today," Dungy said. "But the fumbles, penalties — things that can hurt you — are what happened."

Manning wasn't at a loss to explain the offense's herky-jerky nature against Buffalo.

"When we scored points, we executed," he said.

The Colts took the second half kickoff and moved effortlessly, flawlessly through Buffalo's defense. Manning completed 4-of-5 passes for 48 yards, and Addai completed the nine-play drive with a 5-yard touchdown run.

"When we had turnovers, we didn't execute," Manning said. "When you do that, it can be tough against a defense like that."

Patience was a must. The mistakes nearly ruined the patient approach.

"It's something we have to improve on," Manning said, "but when we had to move the ball and run the clock at the end, we did a good job with that."

Trailing 17-16, Buffalo saw its last chance at an

▲ **WHERE TO GO?** Marvin Harrison looks upfield for some room to run after a second-half catch. He had two catches Sunday for 21 yards. Sam Riche / The Star

upset foiled when Lindell's field goal try drifted wide right.

Six minutes, 22 seconds remained. The Bills' offense never got back on the field.

"Any time you get the ball and you have a chance to kind of seal the victory, that's what you want to do," center Jeff Saturday said. "We came out and did that. You feel good being able to run that much and finish the game."

Addai was the workhorse. He kick-started the game-ending drive with an 8-yard run, then essentially ended the game with a 7-yard run on second-and-4 that generated his third first-down of the drive.

Excluding Manning's two kneel-downs, Addai handled the ball on seven of the eight snaps. He rushed six times for 39 yards and caught a pass for 2 yards.

NO ONE'S PERFECT

Cowboys end Colts' winning streak at 9

By Phil Richards

IRVING, Texas — Peyton Manning reached into his locker and grabbed an orange Gatorade. He took a long, slow drink. The Indianapolis Colts' first loss of the season was a tough one to choke down.

"It's been quite a while since we lost a regular-season road game," he said after turning to face the media mob. "That's why you enjoy the wins. When you lose like this, it rips your guts out."

The team that so consistently has found ways to win, found ways to lose Sunday during a 21-14 stumble against Dallas before 63,706 manic Cowboys fans at Texas Stadium.

The Colts (9-1) had four turnovers in their first loss. They hadn't had more than two in any of their first nine games.

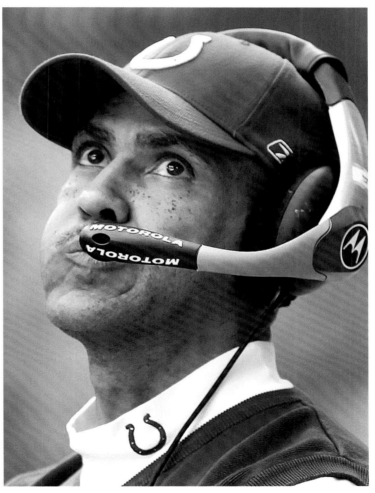

NFL Week Eleven

Cowboys 21
Colts 14

Team record: 9-1

◀**TURNOVERS IN TEXAS:** Cowboys defensive back Roy Williams (left) looks for some running room after picking off a pass in the end zone that was intended for Colts tight end Dallas Clark (44). Sam Riche / The Star

▶**PERFECTION SLIPPING AWAY:** Colts coach Tony Dungy watches as his team falls apart late in the game. Sam Riche / The Star

They hadn't had as many as four in Tony Dungy's previous 73 games as their coach.

"We've had some of this show up in the past and we've been able to dodge bullets," Dungy said. "Today we couldn't dodge a bullet. You play a good team and you make mistakes and it's going to cost you. They did today."

With the cloudless sky looking like a blue ceiling over the stadium, Dallas (6-4) won for the third time in its past four games, handing a loss to the NFL's final unbeaten team. It created opportunities and exploited them. It dominated the fourth quarter 14-0.

The Colts had won seven of their first nine games by seven points or fewer. Five times the margin was five points or less. Three times Manning quarterbacked them to victory on fourth quarter drives.

Not Sunday. The mistakes were too numerous and egregious to overcome.

There were three turnovers during the first 22 minutes.

Wide receiver Marvin Harrison fumbling after a short pass from Manning.

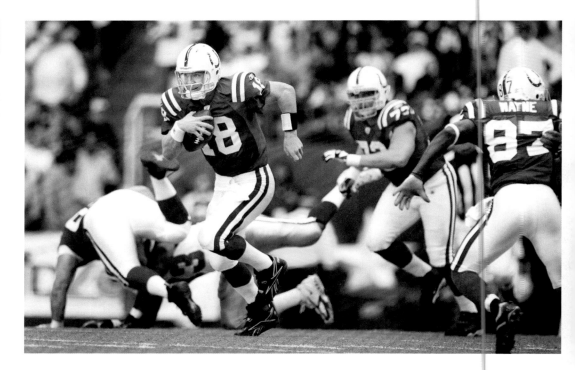

▲ **ON THE RUN:** Colts quarterback Peyton Manning (18) runs for a first down in the first quarter. Sam Riche / The Star

◄ **PICKED UP:** Cato June (59) of the Colts holds his first-half fumble recovery as he runs past Jason Witten of the Cowboys. Robert Scheer / The Star

▲ **HEY OL' BUDDY:** The Colts' Darrell Reid (left) and Raheem Brock (center) jaw at Cowboys kicker Mike Vanderjagt, a former Colt, after he missed a 46-yard field goal attempt in the first half. **Sam Riche** / The Star

◀ **TAKEDOWN:** The Colts' Rob Morris takes down Dallas' Jason Witten in the first half. **Sam Riche** / The Star

Manning fumbling when he was hammered by Cowboys defensive lineman Jay Ratliff.

Safety Roy Williams intercepting a Manning pass while standing directly behind Colts tight end Dallas Clark, who had been knocked to his knees.

And there was another interception when Manning threw into coverage to Harrison and the football was knocked loose by linebacker Kevin Burnett

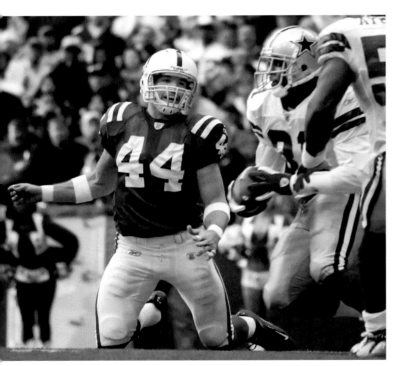

▲ **HEY, THAT'S MINE:** The Cowboys' Roy Williams picks off this pass in the first half in the Cowboys' end zone. The pass was intended for the Colts' Dallas Clark. **Sam Riche** / The Star

▶ **TO RECEPTION:** The Cowboys' Terrell Owens (81) hauls in this pass against the Colts' Nick Harper. **Sam Riche** / The Star

and cornerback Aaron Glenn. Burnett returned his first NFL interception 39 yards for a touchdown.

It was the second turnover returned for a touchdown in as many weeks. Buffalo cornerback Terrence McGee returned a fumble 68 yards during the Colts' 17-16 victory last Sunday.

The Colts overcame their turnovers and other mistakes against the Bills. The Cowboys were a better, tougher team.

▲**RUNNING ROOM:** Joseph Addai rushes during third-quarter action. **Robert Scheer** / The Star

◀**IN FLIGHT:** Reggie Wayne scores a second-quarter touchdown. **Robert Scheer** / The Star

SPORTS

SECTION D • THE INDIANAPOLIS STAR • MONDAY, NOVEMBER 20, 2006 • INDYSTAR.COM/SPORTS

[INSIDE]
Johnson clinches NASCAR title
Jimmie Johnson wins his first Nextel Cup champion-
ship with a ninth-place finish in the season finale **[D2]**
• **PACERS:** Jackson plays through pain. **[D4]**

NFL WEEK 11
COWBOYS 21, COLTS 14

NO ONE'S PERFECT

Cowboys end Colts' winning streak at 9

SLIPPING AWAY: Coach Tony Dungy looks toward the scoreboard.

TURNOVERS IN TEXAS: Cowboys defensive tackle Ray Williams (left) looks for some running room after picking off a pass in the end zone that was intended for Colts tight end Dallas Clark (44). Colts quarterback Peyton Manning, who passed for 254 yards and two touchdowns, threw two interceptions as Indianapolis committed four turnovers. The Cowboys had only two losses.

Suffering a loss could be a blessing in disguise

BOB KRAVITZ

DEFENSE DISINTEGRATES

SMOOTH OPERATOR

NO PANIC

NEXT UP

Turnovers seal fate for NFL's last unbeaten team

By Phil Richards

RAVENS SURGE TO AN 8-2 MARK BY DEFEATING FALCONS 24-10. **D10** | BEARS FINISH OFF SWEEP OF NEW YORK BY STOPPING JETS 10-0. **D10**

JUST 1 MINUTE

SPORTS EDITOR
Jim Lefko
SPORTS PHONE:
317.444.6352

[GO, COLT, GO] AT LEAST THE FOUR-LEGGED PEYTON WON THIS WEEKEND

[ALARM SYSTEM] WHITE'S OK; HOOSIERS ROLL

United Package LIQUORS — *Family of Beverage Shoppes*

▶ **STRETCH FOR IT:** Marvin Harrison (88) makes this fourth-quarter catch against Terence Newman of the Cowboys. Robert Scheer / The Star

---

"Eventually it bites you when you have penalties, have turnovers, do things that are not really within our character," Colts left tackle Tarik Glenn said. "It's a fine line."

Manning tried to squeeze his pass to Harrison through traffic. He's made those throws so many times in the past. Not this time. Glenn and Burnett wouldn't permit it.

Manning's pass to Clark was dead on the money. But Clark wasn't 6-3 as Manning expected. He was half that, kneeling at the Dallas 1.

"I got hit in the back. I don't know how it wasn't a call," Clark said. "It was a good ball. He knocked me down and took my place.

"That was a big one."

Stuff happens, a bunch of it Sunday.

With the Colts leading 14-7 early in the fourth quarter, Dallas faced a third-and-goal from the 10.

Cowboys quarterback Tony Romo threw into the end zone. Colts safety Antoine Bethea intercepted and returned it

104

about 30 yards.

Flags flew. Beaten by wide receiver Terry Glenn, Colts cornerback Jason David had grabbed a fistful of jersey. Defensive holding.

Now it was first-and-goal from the 5. Running back Marion Barber blasted in for the tying touchdown.

Mistakes.

The Colts almost made another comeback. They drove 61 yards to a second-and-3 at the Dallas 9. Running back Joseph Addai was stopped by linebacker Akin Ayodele after a 1-yard gain. Manning threw incomplete to tight end Ben Utectht. On fourth down, with 3:05 to play, he threw incomplete again, this time to Clark.

"They made some plays," Manning said. "They've got a good defense. They made some plays and our offense just wasn't good enough."

The Colts haven't practiced on a Monday in most of a month. Win on Sunday during November and December and you get Monday off is Dungy's deal.

They will practice today, and their thoughts will be on improving, not on the perfect season lost.

"I'll be honest with you," center Jeff Saturday said. "I want to win my division. I want to go to the playoffs. All the rest of it, you can have it. It doesn't make a lot of difference to me. I want to win playoff games."

The Colts can be grateful for that; what they lost Sunday was just a game. ■

▲ **PLAYCALLER:** Dallas coach Bill Parcells signals to one of the players during fourth-quarter action. **Robert Scheer** / The Star

▶ **TAKING CHARGE:** Peyton Manning calls out a play at the line of scrimmage during the fourth quarter.
Robert Scheer / The Star

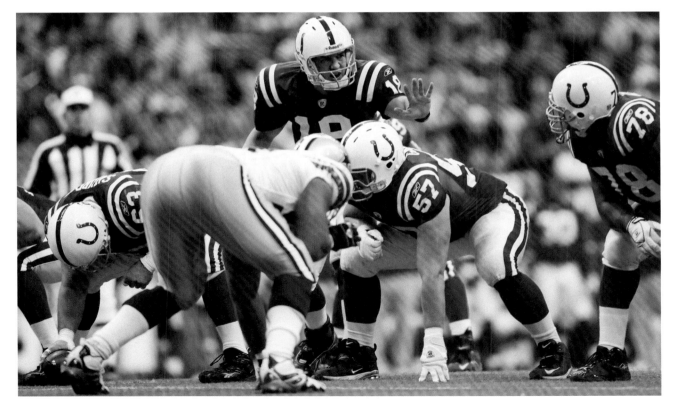

▲ **PREDICTION:** Dallas fans show their allegiance during the game. Robert Scheer / The Star

▶ **DISAPPOINTMENT:** Colts players (from the right) Peyton Manning, Dallas Clark and Brandon Stokley watch the end of the game. Sam Riche / The Star

BOB KRAVITZ'S REPORT CARD

C− RUN OFFENSE: Apparently, there's a reason the Cowboys have the league's third-best overall defense. Even without Greg Ellis, their best pass rusher, they made life miserable for the Colts' offensive line. Neither guy, Joseph Addai nor Dominic Rhodes, ever got things rolling. It would have been nice if Addai could have scored and given the ball to his paralyzed childhood friend, LaJuan Moore, who got to see Addai play in person with the Colts for the first time. Oh, well. It's still a nice story.

C− PASS OFFENSE: You think it doesn't pay to get physical with the Colts' receivers? After the game, a number of Dallas defenders suggested Peyton Manning got rattled, but if anything, I thought the Colts' receivers got rattled. We saw more drops in one game than we've seen all season. The Cowboys did what the Steelers, Patriots and Chargers did in previous seasons. Marvin Harrison had a rare nightmare of a game, but what was more bothersome, he scooted the minute reporters approached his locker. That's not shyness; that's lack of accountability.

B− RUN DEFENSE: For one half and some change, that didn't look like The Worst Run Defense In The NFL. They were better than good; overwhelming, in fact, allowing just 39 yards. In the second half, they wore down slightly, and Julius Jones started gashing them (football term) in the fourth quarter, but the Colts' ability, or inability, to stop the run wasn't the problem Sunday. On a related note, if you read coach Tony Dungy's quotes on Bob Sanders the other day and came away noting he sounded like he was losing his patience with his injured safety, you inferred correctly. I don't know how badly Sanders is hurting, and I will never suggest a guy isn't playing through pain, but there's no question the organization is more than mildly vexed.

C PASS DEFENSE: They were great early and vulnerable late. With the game still in the balance, the slant to Patrick Crayton for a first down finished the job. On another related matter, isn't it time for the Colts to pony up and pay Nick Harper what he's worth? He's a starter making backup money and he's a free agent this summer. And by the way, he's playing some of the best football of his career.

D SPECIAL TEAMS: In the rush to make deadline, I forgot to ask whether Adam Vinatieri's squib kick at the end of the first half was a bad decision or bad execution. I give myself an F for having a brain spasm. But the Colts nearly gave away three charitable points. Another mistake in a day filled with them, although this one didn't come back to bite them. Congratulations to Kelvin Hayden, whose hit on Terence Newman will earn him eternal "Jacked Up" glory.

D COACHING: After the game, Dungy said he never got a suggestion from his coaches upstairs that he should challenge Kevin Burnett's interception. And, home-field advantage being what it is, he never saw a replay on the big screen. But TV replays hinted that Burnett might have been down by contact after picking off the pass. Maybe it would have been overturned and maybe it wouldn't have, but you've got to try there, don't you? As for some late play calls, there was a third-down try on a deep pass to Dallas Clark that brought back memories of the final drive against Pittsburgh.

C− INTANGIBLES: They've won twice in the Meadowlands. They've won in Denver. They've won in Foxborough, Mass. For the first time all season, the Colts looked like the road team, strangely skittish and unsure. But, hey, they'd won nine straight, and there's no reason to think they can't put another big number together. How tough can you be on a team that's 9-1 and still the class of the league?

Addai to remember

Colts rookie runs over Eagles, into franchise record book

By Phil Richards

Indianapolis Colts fans clamoring for more Joseph Addai got what they wanted Sunday evening at the RCA Dome.

Addai right. Addai left. Addai up the middle. Addai in the end zone. Addai in the record book.

The rookie running back tied a club record by rushing for four touchdowns on a night he piled up a career-high 171 yards and a 7.1-yard average on 24 carries as the Colts trampled the Philadelphia Eagles 45-21.

It was quite a show. When Addai took a handoff, started left, then cut off left tackle Tarik Glenn's block on a 4-yard run for his final touchdown and a 38-21 lead, what was left of the sellout crowd of 57,296 stood and roared.

NFL Week Twelve

Colts 45
Eagles 21

Team record: 10-1

◀**PARDON ME WHILE I SCORE:** Colts running back Joseph Addai evades Philadelphia's Matt McCoy (left) and Roderick Hood on the way to his first touchdown. His four touchdowns tied an NFL rookie record. **Matt Detrich** / The Star

▶**NICE JOB:** Joseph Addai (left) is congratulated by his teammates after scoring his fourth touchdown. **Matt Kryger** / The Star

Addai waved; not at the crowd, but at his line. He stood in the end zone and summoned them for a share of the spotlight and a group hug.

"I wanted to share the moment with them and congratulate them on doing such a good job," Addai said.

"He's a team player. He's not a selfish guy," said right guard Jake Scott, who was in on the hug. "He's about trying to help us win and he does that every week."

Addai wasn't the only one who had a good night. The Colts (10-1) bumped their AFC South lead over Jacksonville to four games. They can clinch their fourth consecutive division title by winning Sunday at Tennessee or if the Jaguars lose the same day at Miami.

Philadelphia (5-6) was playing without star quarterback Donovan McNabb, who suffered a season-ending knee injury last week.

Pro Football Hall of Fame member Eric

▶ **HANGING EAGLE:** Colts fan Jeff Seilhamer, Hagerstown, Md., enjoys a beer while a Philadelphia Eagle doll hangs from a tree branch during tailgating before the game. Matt Detrich / The Star

▶▶ **LOOKING FOR AN OPENING:** Colts wide receiver Reggie Wayne tries to elude Eagles defenders Jeremiah Trotter (center) and Sean Considine (right) after a catch in the first quarter. Matt Detrich / The

▲ **READY FOR THE GAME:** Colts fan Gabe Seilhamer, 11, Hagerstown, Md., is dressed and ready for the Colts' game against the Philadelphia Eagles. Matt Detrich / The Star

▶ **GAME NIGHT:** Colts fans start to gather behind the RCA Dome as night sets in before the game. Matt Detrich / The Star

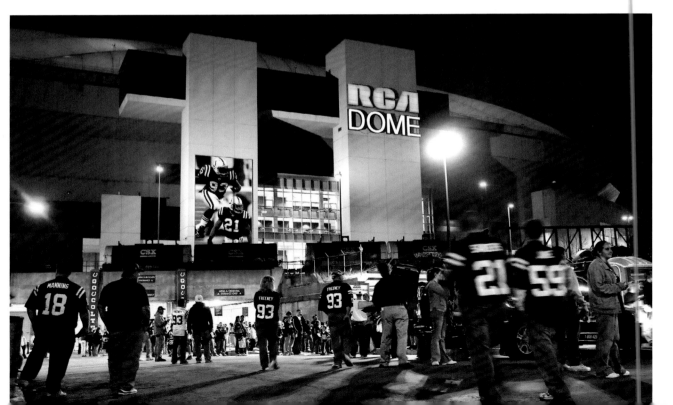

Dickerson is the only other Colt who has rushed for four touchdowns. He did it against Denver on Halloween night in 1988. Seven others have run for three and they include names like Alan Ameche and Lenny Moore, also Hall of Famers, Marshall Faulk, who is headed there, and Edgerrin James, who might be.

Addai exceeded the team's rushing high for this season — 160 yards at the New York Jets on Oct. 1. With Dominic Rhodes rushing 15 times for 68 yards and quarterback Peyton Manning losing 2 on kneeldowns, the Colts

▼ **TD NUMBER TWO:** Indy's Joseph Addai scores his second touchdown of the game. **Sam Riche** / The Star

finished with 237 yards on the ground, their plumpest total since a 275-yard day at Chicago in 2004.

"Joseph ran great," center Jeff Saturday said. "It's obviously fun when you can run the ball like we did tonight."

Call it a coming-out party in Week 12.

Addai has the package. He has great acceleration and makes cuts that are sharp to the point of sudden. He is instinctive, decisive, and at 5-11, 214 pounds, runs with the power of a bigger back. He delivers the blow.

The Colts' first-round draft choice went into the game leading all rookie rushers with 618 yards and a tidy 4.7-yard average despite sharing time with Rhodes.

Addai's highs were 20 carries against the Jets and 93 yards at Denver.

"We want him fresh in December," Colts coach Tony Dungy said, "and you can't argue with the results."

Addai stretched his legs during the first half, when he ran 10 times for 91 yards and three touchdowns.

The Colts took the opening kickoff and blitzed 79 yards in nine plays. Manning was 3-for-4 for 41 yards. Rhodes and Addai shared five carries for 38 yards.

Addai covered the final 15 yards behind blocks from tackles Glenn and Charlie Johnson

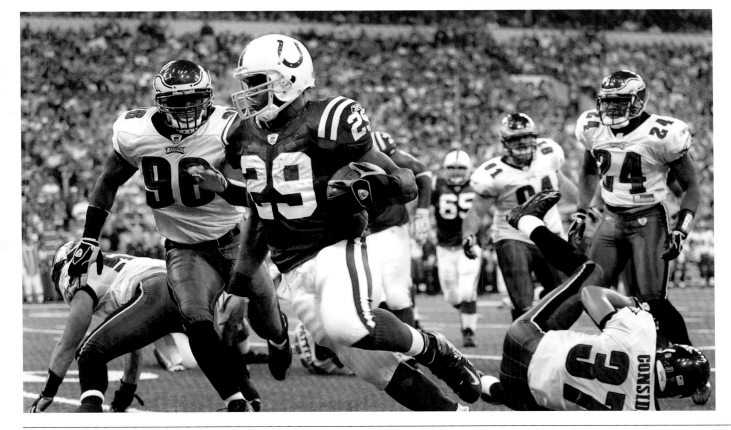

▲ **ON THE LOOSE:** Joseph Addai runs for a first down as Dominic Rhodes (33) cheers from the bench in the second quarter. Matt Kryger / The Star

◄ **TD NUMBER THREE:** Joseph Addai heads to the end zone for his third touchdown of the first half.
Sam Riche / The Star

for the touchdown.

It was the Colts' 10th rushing touchdown of the season and their longest by 9 yards.

The Colts' next two series were more of the same. Addai carried four times for 36 yards, including the final 10 of a 74-yard drive.

He ran four more times for 31 yards, including a second 15-yard touchdown as the Colts marched 60 yards to a 21-0 lead with 8:58 remaining in the first half.

Addai didn't get another touch until the third quarter, but he returned in a lather: five carries for 31 yards and one reception for 21 yards as the Colts pushed their margin to 31-7 with an 89-yard drive that ended with Manning throwing an 11-yard touchdown pass to wide receiver Reggie Wayne.

The thing Dungy liked best about his team's first 100-yard game this season was that it wouldn't turn its owner's head. Addai just plays.

"He won't feel any different tomorrow than he did the first 10 weeks of the season," Dungy promised. ■

▶ **NO RUNNING ROOM:** The Eagles' Brian Westbrook gets hammered in the second half. **Sam Riche** / The Star

▲ **EYES ON THE BALL:** Reggie Wayne catches a touchdown pass from Peyton Manning in the third quarter. **Matt Kryger** / The Star

▲ **JUBILATION:** Colts wide receiver Reggie Wayne celebrates his third-quarter touchdown as a dejected Eagles defense walks off the field. **Matt Detrich** / The Star

◀ **CATCH AND RUN:** Colts tight end Bryan Fletcher tries to outrun Eagles defender Sean Considine after a catch in the third quarter. **Matt Detrich** / The Star

◀◀IT'S A RECORD: Colts running back Joseph Addai (left) breaks into the end zone for his fourth touchdown of the game. Addai's fourth touchdown tied the franchise record for rushing scores in one game, matching Eric Dickerson's mark. The Colts rushed for a season-high 237 yards.

Matt Detrich / The Star

◀ROOKIE COMES OF AGE: Rookie Joseph Addai leaves the field after scoring four touchdowns and rushing for 171 yards. **Sam Riche** / The Star

◀NICE JOB ROOKIE: Colts running back Joseph Addai (left) is congratulated with a tap on the helmet by teammate Ryan Lilja (center) as Tarik Glenn holds up four fingers signifying Addai's fourth touchdown of the night.
Matt Detrich / The Star

▼DECKED OUT AND HAPPY: Dean Lochkovic, Indianapolis, celebrates the Colts' win. **Sam Riche** / The Star

▲ **FUMBLE!:** The Colts' Robert Mathis (left, out of the picture) knocks the ball loose from Eagles quarterback Jeff Garcia for a fumble that the Colts recovered and ran back for a touchdown in the fourth quarter. **Matt Kryger** / The Star

▼ **NO LETTING UP:** Colts coach Tony Dungy yells at an official after a non-call on what Dungy thought was pass interference in the fourth quarter. **Sam Riche** / The Star

▲ **END-ZONE WAVE:** Colts defensive back Kelvin Hayden (right) celebrates with fans and teammates after running back a fumble late in the fourth quarter that put the Colts up 45-21. **Matt Detrich** / The Star

Defense not perfect but limits big plays

By Phillip B. Wilson

Indianapolis Colts outside linebacker Cato June wanted to savor the victory.

That meant no dwelling on any negatives. Even if he initially alluded to one after the Colts downed Philadelphia 45-21 on Sunday night at the RCA Dome.

"Still improving," June said of the defensive effort. "We've just got to learn how to close people out."

That's because the Colts couldn't be satisfied with their defense, even in victory. They again allowed two touchdowns in the second half. The difference this time is it didn't cost them a loss, as it did last week at Dallas.

The Colts had a cushion. The offense produced the big numbers. Until the end of the third quarter, the Colts' defense had done its part, too, allowing just seven points.

But the Eagles scored in the final seconds of the third, then added another score in the fourth to close to 31-21. The game was still in doubt.

And it's not like the Eagles were themselves. Once a big-play offense, the visitors were reduced by the loss of quarterback Donovan McNabb to a season-ending injury last week to just throwing short. In other words, with Jeff Garcia taking snaps, these were the "dink-and-dunk" Eagles.

That meant a lot of running plays. That meant a lot of short passes. Garcia completed 19-of-23 passes but for just 140 yards. His longest completion was 19 yards.

The Colts allowed few long gains, but they also allowed drives of 14, 10 and 11 plays. At the end, the Colts came up with a couple of late fumble recoveries, the first of which Robert Mathis forced and Kelvin Hayden took 26 yards for Indianapolis' final score. That culminated what looked like a rout from the final score, but was not yet secure until late in the game.

Three turnovers, one touchdown scored — both good things for Colts defenders. The 21 points allowed, however, were not so good.

"That's way too many. That's definitely too many points," said cornerback Nick Harper, who had a second-quarter interception.

"We knew they weren't going to test us down the field and they didn't. It was one of those games where we knew it was going to be a short, quick game. There were some routes I wanted to jump but didn't."

The Eagles entered with a league-high 54 plays gaining 20 yards or more. This night, they had only one. Running back Brian Westbrook broke off a 21-yard run late in the second quarter.

The Eagles were also best in the NFL with 20 pass plays gaining 30 yards or more. But this night, without McNabb, they had none.

Westbrook rushed for 124 yards on 20 carries, 6.2 per rush, on the league's worst run defense. The Eagles averaged 6 yards per carry with 149 yards on 25 attempts.

"He got a couple good plays on us," middle linebacker Gary Brackett said of Westbrook, "but for the most part we were able to contain him."

Brackett, who led the team with eight total

▲ **TAKEDOWN:** Colts defensive back Jason David drags down the Eagles' Thomas Tapeh during first-half action. **Sam Riche** / The Star

tackles, later admitted the Colts need to clean up their tackling.

Mathis, who forced fumbles with both of his sacks, conceded there's improvement to be made.

"We're still a work in progress," he said. "We've just got to hone in on our techniques and get better every week."

But did he depart the RCA Dome feeling better about the defense?

"I feel better about a win in general," Mathis said.

KICK TO THE GUT

Bironas' long boot sends Colts to dispiriting defeat

By Phil Richards

NASHVILLE, Tenn. — Midway through the second quarter Sunday, the Indianapolis Colts had a 14-point lead and a chance to recover a Tennessee fumble. First the football got away, then the game.

Rob Bironas kicked a 60-yard field goal that rode a 10-15 mph north wind through the cool December sunshine to split the uprights with seven seconds to play and beat the stumbling Colts 20-17. LP Field's sellout crowd of 69,143 went home smiling, witnesses of a kick that tied for the fourth longest in the NFL's 87-year history.

The Colts left wondering. While the Titans (5-7) spent the afternoon making plays, the Colts (10-2) spent it making mistakes. They have lost two of their past three games and fallen into a tie with San Diego in the chase for the

NFL Week Thirteen

Titans 20
Colts 17

Team record: 10-2

◄**BIG BOOT:** Titans David Stewart (76) and Jacob Bell (60) celebrate a 60-yard field goal by kicker Rob Bironas (2) to defeat the Colts 20-17 at LP Field in Nashville, Tenn. Matt Kryger / The Star

▶**NOWHERE TO RUN:** Dominic Rhodes is tackled by the Titans' Keith Bulluck (53) in the first quarter. Matt Kryger / The Star

AFC's No. 1 playoff seed.

"The two games we've lost have been the same M.O.," Colts coach Tony Dungy said. "We go on the road, we have penalties, we have turnovers, we give up long drives because we're not real crisp on defense.

"And we had plenty of chances."

Dungy now is 61-1 as an NFL head coach when his teams take a 14-point lead. He hasn't had a defense quite like this one.

A victory would have clinched the AFC South championship and the Colts' seventh trip to the playoffs in eight seasons.

Instead, the Colts were waving at Tennessee quarterback Vince Young and bouncing off Titans running back Travis Henry. They couldn't get a hand on the former. They couldn't get their arms around the latter. Tennessee ran 35 times for 219 yards, a 6.3-yard average. Young ran nine times for 78 yards. Six of his scrambles and draws converted third downs.

"We tackle better on first and second down and we're off the field," Colts linebacker and co-captain Gary Brackett said.

The lapses weren't the sole province of the defense.

There were four false starts, a touchdown

▲ CLEVER KID: Colts fan Jake Sprool, Columbia, Tenn., cheers on the Colts at the start of their game. Matt Kryger / The Star

▶ GO COLTS!: Colts fans Adam Goodwin (left) Chris Chisler (center) and David D'Angelo, all from Indianapolis, cheer on the Colts. Matt Kryger / The Star

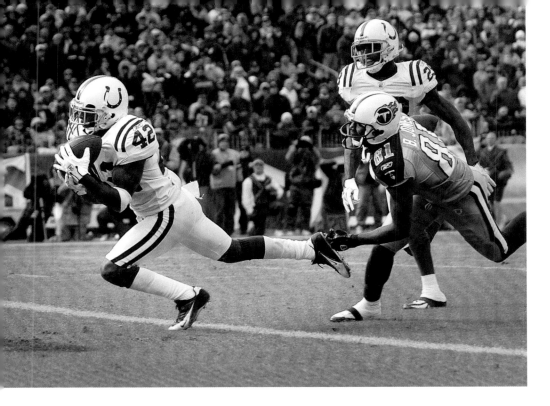

▲**NICE PICK:** Jason David (42) intercepts a Vince Young pass in the first quarter. **Matt Kryger** / The Star

nullified by a penalty, dropped passes, two turnovers. The Colts scored three points over the final 37 minutes.

Quarterback Peyton Manning completed 21-of-28 passes for 351 yards and a touchdown but two of his passes were bobbled by his receivers and intercepted by the Titans. Wide receiver Marvin Harrison, who caught seven passes for 172 yards and a touchdown, had one bobble. Tight end Bryan Fletcher had the other.

"We had some chances. We had some plays where we just

▲**HEADED FOR THE END ZONE:** Marvin Harrison brings in this first-quarter touchdown. **Robert Scheer** / The Star

◀**GIFTED RUNNER:** Titans quarterback Vince Young puts a move on the Colts' Cato June in the first quarter. **Matt Kryger** / The Star

execute," Manning said. "That's kind of a boring answer, but that's usually what it comes down to."

Running back Dominic Rhodes blasted 2 yards for the touchdown that put the Colts up 14-0. Rocky Boiman knocked the ball loose on the ensuing kickoff, but Tennessee's Eugene Amano recovered.

The Titans then scored 10 points in the span of 1:38 during the final two minutes of the first half.

Tennessee led 17-14 when, on first-and-goal at the Titans 1, Colts running back Joseph Addai took a handoff and darted left. The blocking broke down. Titans linebacker Keith Bulluck and tackle Albert Haynesworth buried Addai for a 1-yard loss.

On second down, Manning threw to tight end Ben Utecht for the go-ahead touchdown. A penalty flag flew. Utecht was penalized for offensive pass interference. He and safety Chris Hope had collided in the end zone.

"It was a huge surprise to me," Utecht said. "Contact's part of the game. We butted heads about 5 or 6 yards deep in the end zone and I had to get loose. I peeled off and got open."

The Colts settled for a tying field goal.

That's how it went.

"Games are starting to matter more and you've got to elevate your game," Colts tackle Ryan Lilja said. "You know your opponent's going to do that."

Two of the past three weeks, the Colts haven't. They've had more errors than answers. ■

▶**NOT THIS TIME:** The Colts' pitch-and-catch tandem of Peyton Manning and Marvin Harrison may be the most prolific in NFL history, but on this play Manning's throw was intercepted by Titans linebacker Peter Sirmon. **Matt Kryger** / The Star

MY BAD: Brandon Stokley was frustrated after dropping a pass as the Titans' Chris Hope (left) defended in the third quarter. Matt Kryger / The Star

▼ **THIS ISN'T GOOD:** Colts coach Tony Dungy and Darrell Reid look up at the scoreboard in the third quarter.
Matt Kryger / The Star

▲ **TOO MUCH CELEBRATING:** Marlin Jackson (28) celebrates with Robert Mathis (98) after Jackson intercepted a Vince Young pass in the third quarter. Jackson was flagged on this play for excessive celebration. Matt Kryger / The Star

BOB KRAVITZ'S REPORT CARD

C–ⁿ RUN OFFENSE: At some point in every season, it seems the Colts' inability to run in short-yardage situations bites them in the derriere. This game, it happened twice. With third-and-1 at the Tennessee 37 and 10:49 left in the game, Joseph Addai was thrown for a 2-yard loss. They punt. Later, the Colts had first-and-goal at the Tennessee 1-yard line and were poised to take a 21-17 lead with three or four minutes left. Addai, again, was stuffed, followed by an offensive pass interference (please, no whining), an incompletion and a Peyton Manning scramble. They kick a field goal. If I'm the Colts, I've got a big, bruising fullback on my Christmas gift list.

B– PASS OFFENSE: Two pieces of good news: One, Marvin Harrison came back with a big game after some early mishaps, including a tipped pass that turned into an interception. And two, the Colts didn't lose this time to a 3-4 defense, so that's progress. Peyton Manning got his numbers, but there were too many drops, too many false start penalties and that Keith Bulluck interception before halftime was a game-changer. It's a little bit hard to grade on such incomplete information; the Colts' offense only had the ball three times in the second half.

D RUN DEFENSE: I would give this group an "F," but when it comes to Vince Young's heroics on the ground, I'm going to save some of the vitriol for the pass defense. Hey, it's my Dopey Report Card and I'll do what I want. The basic problem, best I can tell, is the Colts can't tackle anybody. I'm sorry, but Gilbert Gardner has broken team president Bill Polian's streak of successfully replacing free agent linebackers with better, cheaper in-house talent. I mean, 6.3 yards per carry is embarrassing. When did Travis Henry become Jim Brown?

D PASS DEFENSE: I don't know all there is to know about various pass coverages and techniques, but I know that when the opponent is at the 8-yard line, the defender — let's just call him Jason David — should not be 10 yards off the ball. The bigger issue, though, was the Colts' failure to figure out a way to do anything with Young's scrambling, especially on third down. He made it look like last year's national final against USC, didn't he? Worse yet, it appeared the Colts were confused about what they were supposed to be doing defensively almost all day.

C SPECIAL TEAMS: Adam Vinatieri's 53-yard miss just before halftime didn't seem like that big a deal at the time. But when Rob Bironas' wind-aided 60-yarder gave the Titans a three-point win, the Vinatieri miss came back into focus. It's weird how all season, opposing field goal kickers have been ridiculously off-target against the Colts. Then Bironas, who was back on the field after the game, taking pictures with his family from midfield, knocks one through from 60. Go figure.

D– COACHING: I'll spare you further comment on the misguided Tony Dungy timeout near the end of the game. If you need to read more about it, take a look at my column again. But that wasn't the only demerit. The Colts defense seemed confused all day, and the Colts defensive coaches never seemed to find a way to slow Young. Offensively, they also seemed to get a little bit conservative once they got the 14-0 lead, which is really out of character for this team.

D INTANGIBLES: Sorry. No intangibles from this game. It's my week to mope.

◄ **DESPERATION:** Peyton Manning launches a long pass to Marvin Harrison in the fourth quarter.
Matt Kryger / The Star

▼ **FRUSTRATION:** Peyton Manning walks off the field after losing to the Tennessee Titans 20-17.
Matt Kryger / The Star

Colts feeling rundown

By Mike Chappell

NASHVILLE, Tenn. — Vince Young and the Tennessee Titans spent Sunday afternoon running roughshod through Indianapolis' generous defense.

The Colts clearly had no answers during the game — they yielded 219 yards on 35 attempts, a withering 6.3 per-carry average — or afterward.

"This is no different than any other game we win or lose," defensive end Dwight Freeney said after the Colts did the latter, falling to the Titans 20-17. "We've got to go back and look at the tape."

What, again?

Tennessee pulled the upset on Rob Bironas' 60-yard field goal with seven seconds remaining. But making his dramatic kick possible was a problem that has plagued the Colts since they opened the season against the New York Giants more than three months ago.

They couldn't stop the run Sept. 10 in Giants Stadium, couldn't stop it against the Titans on Oct. 8 in the RCA Dome, couldn't stop it at Denver on Oct. 29 and, well, you get the idea.

It's a broken record that features a defense that either is broken or unfixable to this point.

Asked if the defense is getting any better, Freeney replied: "I would think so. We're not getting any worse, I know that. We just have to make some more plays."

Young presented a unique problem: an athletic, 6-4, 233-pound quarterback who doesn't hesitate to tuck the football and run. As the Colts primarily played zone, he allowed the linebackers and defensive backs to drop into coverage, side-stepped the rush of the front four and took off. He finished with 78 yards on nine scrambles.

Tennessee converted 8-of-13 times on third down. Young accounted for six of the conversions by stepping out of tackles and scampering for the necessary yardage, and then some. His six third-down rushes netted 58 yards.

"I can imagine how frustrated (the Colts) are, but that's why he's here," Titans coach Jeff Fisher said. "He kept drives alive for us."

Young, though, had plenty of help. Travis Henry pounded away at the Colts 20 times for 93 yards. Rookie LenDale White had 35 yards on just four carries.

Young said the Titans were able to use the Colts' up-the-field rush by the defensive line to their advantage.

"That's what they do and that's what they teach," he said. "They try to let the linebackers make the plays and (Bob) Sanders and the free safety make the plays."

The Colts were quick to credit Young, Henry, whichever Titan had success against them. But they also insisted on shouldering much of the blame for another porous, inconsistent afternoon. Of the Titans' 35 rushes, seven gained at least 11 yards. Three went for at least 26.

There were too many missed tackles, too many whiffs when it came to corralling Young.

"It's definitely us," said Sanders, who returned to the lineup after missing the past three games with soreness in his right knee. "That's not Colts football. That's not what we do. That's not how we play."

But it has been. The Colts are giving up 159.9

▲ **ROOM TO RUN:** Titans quarterback Vince Young, who ran nine times for 78 yards, scrambles through the Colts defense for a first down in the third quarter. Matt Kryger / The Star

yards per game, 5.1 yards per attempt. They've now allowed at least 200 rushing yards three times in the past eight games.

Defensive tackle Anthony McFarland wanted no part of any complicated postgame analysis. The problem, he said, is as basic as blocking and tackling.

"Obviously you have to give credit to them," he said. "Any time you've got a great athlete at quarterback, he's another weapon. But some of it is probably on us, poor tackling. It's something we've just got to get corrected."

RUN OUT OF TOWN

Jaguars crush Colts with 375 rushing yards

By Phil Richards

JACKSONVILLE, Fla. — Nothing short of injury or exhaustion was going to stop running backs Fred Taylor and Maurice Jones-Drew on Sunday at sold-out Alltel Stadium. The Indianapolis Colts' feeble defense certainly couldn't.

The Colts were little more than speed bumps as Jacksonville ran for 375 yards and four touchdowns while trampling the visitors 44-17 on a mild, sunny north Florida afternoon.

Only once since the 1970 AFL/NFL merger has a team rushed for more yards, according to Elias Stats Bureau: Cincinnati totaled 407 against Denver on Oct. 22, 2000.

Taylor rushed nine times for 131 yards, a 14.6-yard average, and one touchdown before pulling up with a sore hamstring late during the first half.

Jones-Drew ran 15 times for 166 yards and two touchdowns.

◀ **SUDDENLY SKIDDING:** Quarterback Peyton Manning sits dejectedly on the bench late in the Colts' second straight loss. **Matt Detrich** / The Star

▶ **RUNNING FREE:** Jaguars running back Fred Taylor (right) spins away from the Colts' Marlin Jackson in the first quarter. **Matt Kryger** / The Star

NFL Week Fourteen

Jaguars 44
Colts 17

Team record: 10-3

He also returned a kickoff 93 yards for another touchdown before taking a seat during the third quarter. If Jones-Drew wasn't exhausted, he should have been.

"Those guys ran through us, and it started from play one and went all through the game," Colts coach Tony Dungy said.

"The thing I told the team is, 'We're going to see what we're made of from here.'"

Sunday was a continuation of the tired litany of missed assignments, missed tackles, miscommunication and missed opportunity. A victory would have clinched the AFC South title.

Instead, the Colts lost for the third time in the past four games and suffered their worst regular-season defeat since a 41-6 battering at Miami on Dec. 10, 2001.

Jacksonville (8-5) needed to win to boost its playoff hopes, and played like it.

With the Colts (10-3) confused about what defense they were playing, Taylor darted through the middle, broke a tackle by safety Antoine Bethea, and bolted 76 yards on the Jaguars' first play from scrimmage. Jones-Drew went 18 yards for a touchdown on the second.

"Haywire" was the word Dungy used to describe his team's performance.

Colts receivers dropped three of quarterback Peyton Manning's first four passes. The Jaguars blocked a Hunter Smith punt and averaged 47.3 yards on three kickoff returns. The Colts averaged 1.7 yards on 20 rushes; they were outrushed 375-34.

They didn't block or tackle or execute on offense. They didn't play. If no one is hitting the panic button, maybe someone should.

"We've got to step it up. Ain't nowhere else to go," linebacker Gary Brackett said.

"Talking is one thing. We're kind of in a 'show me' mode as opposed to talking about it," quarterback Peyton Manning said.

"You can't just say things are going to get

▲ **PAINTED AND READY:** Colts fan Austin Keele, 6, Indianapolis, watches the team get ready for the game. Matt Kryger / The Star

▶ **BOLD STATEMENT:** Denese McLarty, Palm Bay, Fla., waves at the Colts' Dwight Freeney as her husband Scott (right) and Trevor Steele, New Palestine, Ind., look on. Matt Kryger / The Star

better, they're going to get fixed. You have to go out and do it."

Manning completed 25-of-50 passes for 313 yards with one interception. Wide receiver Reggie Wayne caught eight passes for 110 yards and Marvin Harrison had six receptions for 101 yards. Harrison became the fourth player in NFL history with 1,000 receptions by pushing his total to 1,001.

Those were the highlights, and no one was talking about them.

Bethea talked about how the Colts knew the Jaguars were going to run and their primary focus was to stop it.

"Go back and look at it," nose tackle Anthony "Booger" McFarland urged. "We'll have guys sitting right there to make the tackles. We'll have

KRAVITZ ON THE COLTS

The only reason the Jaguars didn't go for 400 yards Sunday was the end zone kept getting in the way.

This is not the time for more stay-the-course rhetoric. Panic? You know, a little bit of panic might not be the worst thing right now. Those obscene running numbers ... virtually demand a helping of panic.

guys on the tackle, but we missed."

The Colts have said the same things week after week: after yielding 186 rushing yards to the New York Giants, 191 to Jacksonville in the teams' first meeting, 214 and 219 to Tennessee and 227 to Denver.

Dungy held out hope. Even better, he held out an example.

"I've been in this situation before and actually had a much worse loss than this when we were in the middle of a playoff run at Tampa," said Dungy, who coached the Buccaneers from 1996 through 2001. "We lost a game 45-0 and it wasn't even this good and we came back and went to the championship game."

Sure enough, in 1999. The loss came at Oakland during Week 15. The Bucs won their final two regular-season games. They beat Washington in a divisional playoff game before falling at St. Louis 11-6 in the NFC Championship Game.

Strange things happen. The Colts are banking on it. ■

▲ **GOOD FOR THREE:** Colts kicker Adam Vinatieri boots a field goal as punter Hunter Smith holds the ball in the first quarter. **Matt Detrich** / The Star

◄**TALKING IT OVER:** Peyton Manning talks with offensive coordinator Tom Moore on the sidelines in the second quarter. **Matt Detrich** / The Star

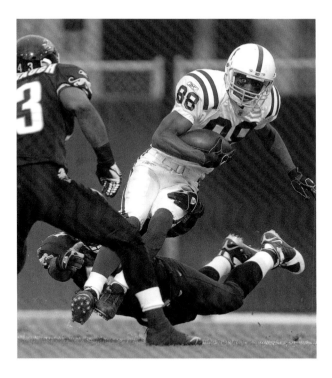

▶ **MAKING A MOVE:** The Colts' Marvin Harrison looks to avoid a couple Jaguars tacklers in the third quarter. **Matt Kryger** / The Star

▶▶ **HIGH FLYER:** Robert Mathis (98) dives over the line in an attempt to block a field goal in the third quarter. **Matt Kryger** / The Star

▼ **SO CLOSE:** Reacting to a near Colts touchdown are (left to right) Dick Boshen, Mike Bowman, Kitty Bowman, Judy Boshen and Audrey Rawnsley. The Colts' fans gathered at the home of Mike Bowman in Indianapolis to watch the game. **Rob Goebel** / The Star

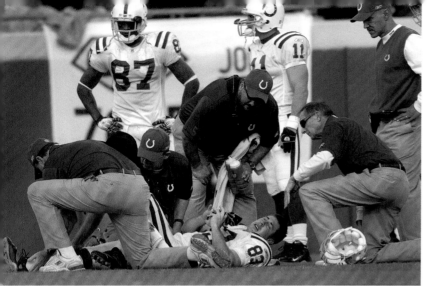

▲ **INJURY TIME OUT:** Colts wide receiver Brandon Stokley is attended to by the Colts medical staff after he injured his right ankle in the third quarter.
Matt Kryger / The Star

▶ **HE'S DONE:** Brandon Stokley is helped off the field after the play.
Matt Kryger / The Star

▶ **LONG WALK:** The Colts walk into the locker room after losing to the Jacksonville Jaguars 44-17. Matt Kryger / The Star

▲ DISAPPOINTMENT: Defensive end Robert Mathis sits dejectedly on the bench in the fourth quarter. Matt Kryger / The Star

◄ THIS HURTS: Brandon Stokley sits behind the Colts' bench with his right ankle in a walking boot. Matt Kryger / The Star

BOB KRAVITZ'S REPORT CARD

F RUN OFFENSE: Before we get much further in this week's Dopey Report Card, a quick word to those of you who have a weak stomach or a tender constitution: This week's DRC isn't going to be pretty. We're talking Quentin Tarantino-quality grisly. But, then, if you made it through Sunday's game without incident, this might not seem so bad. Running game? Couple of negative plays early, and it kept getting worse. I can't even make my weekly Joseph-Addai-needs-more-carries argument. P.S., I lo-o-ove that stretch play.

D PASS OFFENSE: Never before in the DRC's short and undistinguished history have I awarded a "D" to a passing game that produced more than 300 yards. Bottom line, when that was still a competitive game, they didn't get it done. The first offensive drive set the tone: an underthrown (maybe wind-blown) pass to Marvin Harrison that could have been seven, then a drop by Brandon Stokley in the end zone. Once they go into desperation mode, it turned ugly. P.S., I lo-o-ove that halfback option.

F RUN DEFENSE: In recent weeks, I've received notes from kind readers wondering why I've held back from giving the run defense an "F" after some recent lackluster performances. Well, this was why. Because I had the disquieting sense that things could get worse, much worse, and if you drop an "F" on them after giving up 200-something, what do you do when an opponent goes for 375? Give them a "T"? Right now, Cincinnati running back Rudi Johnson could gain 100 next week even if half of his offensive teammates are in jail.

INC. PASS DEFENSE: Pass defense? What pass defense? Nobody even bothers anymore. The Colts put 10 guys in the box and opponents still pound them senseless. I'm just telling you now, if the Bengals offensive coaches even attempt to pass the ball the first few possessions a week from tonight, they should all be fired immediately. Or at least have their coaching licenses revoked. Something.

F SPECIAL TEAMS: The only reason special teams coach Russ Purnell isn't getting all the heat today is because defensive coordinator Ron Meeks is on the staff. But his group didn't cover itself in glory, either. Hunter Smith had a nightmare day punting. And there was a blocked punt. And a kick returned for a touchdown by Maurice Jones-Drew. And, well, what am I telling you for? Yeah, injuries are killing the special teams. But everybody has injuries in December. That was brutal.

F COACHING: OK, I've already made my case with the defense, the way the defensive ends take themselves out of the play, etc. At this point, I want to know why in heaven's name Peyton Manning was still on the field in the final minutes of a lost game. When I asked Dungy after the game, he said he wanted to get something going, which makes no sense at any level. What if Manning takes a freak hit to the knee or steps incorrectly on the turf? To get something going in a 44-17 game? If I'm Jim Sorgi, I want to know what it's going to take to get into a game. Maybe if he said he could tackle.

F INTANGIBLES: The last time we visited the "intangibles" section after a game against the Jaguars, we were escorted and amused by former Vice President in Charge of Intangibles, Hunter Smith. That's when he shared that great line about the Jaguars' lack of class and sophistication. It was, not so coincidentally, the last time Hunter worked for me in that capacity. In fairness, then, I should note that the Colts were the ones who were losing their composure down the stretch.

FLYING HIGH AGAIN

Colts click on both offense and defense

By Phil Richards

Like any well-formulated offense, the Indianapolis Colts took what was given them Monday night at the RCA Dome: mostly dinks and dump-offs, pops to the running back, quick slants, short stuff over the middle, and yes, four touchdowns and a desperately needed 34-16 victory.

Peyton Manning completed 29-of-36 passes for 282 yards and four touchdowns in a lethally efficient performance that kept the sell-out crowd of 57,292 coming out of its seats.

The Colts (11-3) had lost their previous two games and three of four since a 9-0 start. With a game at Houston (4-10) on Sunday, they have a chance to build a little momentum.

Handed the AFC South title Sunday by Jacksonville's loss at Tennessee, the Colts got in the season's spirit. Their victory

NFL Week Fifteen

Colts 34
Bengals 16

Team record: 11-3

◄**MARVELOUS YET AGAIN:** Colts wide receiver Marvin Harrison (88) slips away from Bengals defender Deltha O'Neal after a third-quarter catch. Harrison had three touchdowns among his eight catches. Sam Riche / The Star

▶**RISING TO THE OCCASION:** Reggie Wayne (87) celebrates his third-quarter touchdown with teammates Tarik Glenn (78) and Dominic Rhodes. It was Wayne's ninth touchdown of the season. Sam Riche / The Star

dump-off and a pass sailed through Harrison's hands on the next play, but Manning's receivers had almost as good a day as he did.

Manning hit 18-of-20 passes for 148 yards and two touchdowns during a stunning first-half display of accuracy.

Cincinnati's lone touchdown was set up when Terrence Wilkins muffed a Bengals punt at the Colts 25-yard line. Running back Rudi Johnson ran through safety Dexter Reid's tackle to score from the 12. ■

▶ **FREENEY FOR THE DEFENSE:** Colts defensive end Dwight Freeney (93) sacks Bengals quarterback Carson Palmer, causing a fumble on Cincinnati's first drive. The Colts scored a field goal after the fumble recovery. **Matt Kryger** / The Star

▶ **TALKIN' TRASH:** The Colts' Dwight Freeney celebrates his first-quarter sack. **Sam Riche** / The Star

▶▶ **FIRST BLOOD:** Colts kicker Adam Vinatieri delivers a field goal for the first score of the game. **Matt Detrich** / The Star

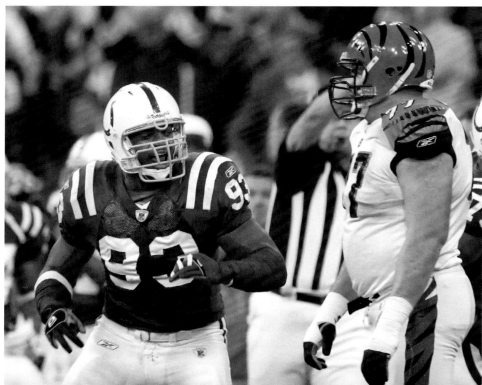

▲ **ROAR!:** Rocky Boiman (50) of the Colts reacts after a play in the second quarter. **Matt Detrich** / The Star

▶ **RUN, RUN, RUN!:** Colts quarterback Peyton Manning breaks away for a first down in the second quarter. **Matt Detrich** / The Star

KRAVITZ ON THE COLTS

After all the madness, after the nine straight wins and the three losses in four games, after being anointed as the Super Bowl favorite and being dismissed as a Super Bowl afterthought that is doomed to an early demise, here's where the Indianapolis Colts are as they prepare for Houston and a chance to hold down the No. 2 playoff spot:

They're right where they want to be.

Well, OK, sitting on a beach in Kauai and nursing a mai tai is exactly where they want to be, but in terms of playoff positioning, the Colts really couldn't be in a more favorable spot this time around.

▲ON THE RUN: Reggie Wayne heads upfield after a third-quarter catch. **Sam Riche** / The Star

◀◀SWARMING: Colts defenders Dwight Freeney (93), Darrell Reid (95), Rob Morris (arm on ball carrier) and Nick Harper (25) team up to tackle Bengals running back Rudi Johnson. **Sam Riche** / The Star

◀TEAMWORK REWARDED: Peyton Manning and Marvin Harrison celebrate their third touchdown combo of the night. **Matt Kryger** / The Star

▲ **FAN RECOGNITION:** Reggie Wayne points to the fans after the Colts defeated the Bengals. **Matt Kryger** / The Star

▼ **HAPPY DAYS ARE HERE AGAIN:** Colts fans scream for their team as they lead the Bengals 34-16 late in the fourth quarter. **Matt Detrich** / The Star

▲ **MORE HEAT:** Colts defensive end Dwight Freeney slams into Bengals quarterback Carson Palmer.

Matt Kryger / The Star

▶ **LAST RUN:** The Colts' Joseph Addai gets 41 yards on this run, which was the last of the game for him. He sprained his ankle on the play.

Sam Riche / The Star

Colts end their slump with by-the-book perfection

By Mike Chappell

The blueprint for how the Indianapolis Colts must maneuver through the playoffs was on display for everyone to see Monday night in the RCA Dome.

Playing in front of a sellout crowd and a national TV audience that undoubtedly included other playoff hopefuls, the Colts regained their sense of direction. They blended an efficient, productive offense with an attacking, surer-tackling defense. The result: a 34-16 victory over the Cincinnati Bengals that got everyone's attention.

It certainly got Tony Dungy's.

"We've got a team that's capable of beating anybody," the Colts coach said Tuesday afternoon. "When we play well, we can."

In their 44-17 drubbing at Jacksonville the previous weekend, the Colts were thoroughly outclassed, from offense to defense to special teams to coaching. Their bounce-back performance against the Bengals was just as complete in a positive sense.

The offense and defense, quarterback Peyton Manning said, "kind of fed off each other."

It's that type of complementary play that could enable the Colts to make a serious push for their first Super Bowl appearance since their Baltimore brethren reached the championship game after the 1970 regular season.

By winning their last two games, beginning with Sunday's trip to Houston, the Colts (11-3) assure themselves no worse than a No. 2 seed and a first-round bye. They are a long shot to overtake San Diego (12-2) for the No. 1 seed.

A first-round bye, noted Dungy, "means you've only got to win two games (to get to the Super Bowl). But it's always been about momentum ... it's how you're playing."

Against the Bengals, the Colts were on top of their game.

The Manning-led offense played error-free for the first time in nearly two months, and finished what it started. After settling for Adam Vinatieri's 30-yard field goal on its first trip inside the Bengals 20-yard line, the offense went 4-for-4.

"Just a real mind-set," said Manning, whose four touchdown passes were delivered in the red zone.

That contributed to the Colts settling into a 24-13 lead in the third quarter. It marked only the sixth game in which they earned a double-digit cushion. Last season, double-digit leads were common, occurring in 11 of their first 13 games.

Armed with the lead and intent on tightening up its sloppy tackling, the defense enjoyed one of its most complete games. It allowed the Bengals to convert just 2-of-11 third-down situations and limited them to three field goals and one touchdown on four red-zone possessions.

More important, the defense was able to play to its strengths. While the Bengals had a modicum of success on the ground against the Colts' No. 32-ranked run defense — 133 yards, 4.4 yards per attempt — they were unable to keep the pass rush from engulfing quarterback Carson Palmer.

▲ **WRAPPING HIM UP:** Colts linebacker Rob Morris (94) stops Rudi Johnson on a third-quarter run. **Matt Detrich** / The Star

"We did what we had to do and set the tone early," defensive end Dwight Freeney said.

Cincinnati's first possession ended when Freeney beat rookie left tackle Andrew Whitworth and stripped the ball from Palmer. It was the first of three Freeney sacks, each of which forced a fumble. The Colts finished with four sacks of Palmer, who seldom had time to look downfield for Chad Johnson and T.J. Houshmandzadeh.

In the end, it was a lot of offense, a lot of defense and just enough special teams.

"That's how you have to play to beat good teams," Dungy said.

Bye-bye to playoff bye?

Lowly Texans stun defenseless Colts

By Phil Richards

HOUSTON — After a week of talking about building play-off momentum, the Indianapolis Colts went out and made some noise Sunday at Reliant Stadium.

Thud.

"We had our fate in our hands," Colts safety Marlin Jackson said, "and we dropped it."

Kris Brown kicked a 48-yard field goal on the game's final play to give Houston a 27-24 victory that rendered the Colts' prospects for the AFC's No. 2 playoff seed and the attendant first-round bye a long shot.

If they are to get a bye, the Colts (11-4) must beat Miami (6-8) in their regular-season finale Sunday at the RCA Dome, and Baltimore (12-3) must lose at home to Buffalo (7-8).

The Colts have issues far more fundamental than playoff

◄ **WALKING AWAY:** Colts defensive tackle Darrell Reid has a long walk back to the locker room by himself after a field goal on the game's final play beat the Colts.
Matt Detrich / The Star

► **HMM, THIS ISN'T GOOD:** Colts quarterback Peyton Manning glances at the scoreboard in the third quarter. Matt Kryger / The Star

NFL Week Sixteen

Texans 27
Colts 24

Team record: 11-4

seeding. They have lost four of six games since a 9-0 start. They have lost four in succession on the road for the first time since 2001.

It was the second time in four weeks that they fell on a last-play field goal.

"We didn't lose that game on a last-second field goal," protested Colts linebacker Rob Morris, mindful of another tired four-quarter episode of missed tackles, blown assignments and the defense's utter inability to make third-down stops and give the offense opportunities.

"I've been on a team that finished 6-10 and this is not a time to get ready for next year," Morris said. "It's not the time to panic, not the time to fold. We've got to go home, look in the mirror, come out next week, play with some heart, get some momentum. It's the only option, really, right now."

For the record, Tennessee's Rob Bironas kicked a 60-yard bomb to beat the Colts 20-17 on Dec. 3 in Nashville. That game was the same story: A Colts defense that yielded 8-of-13 third-down conversions and 219 rushing yards.

The defense permitted 191 rushing yards Sunday — nearly double the Texans' average — and conversions on 10 of Houston's 14 third downs.

Houston (5-10) had lost four of its previous five games. It didn't play like it.

Running back Ron Dayne was a 245-pound cannon ball. He shot through huge gaps, often untouched by the Colts' defensive linemen and linebackers, and hurtled into the secondary. Safeties Marlin Jackson and Antoine Bethea had 23 tackles, 14 by Jackson. No wonder Colts safeties have so many injury issues.

▲ **TIGHTEN UP:** Colts quarterback Peyton Manning has his cleats changed by the Colts assistant equipment manager Sean Sullivan (left) before the the the game. **Matt Kryger** / The Star

▶ **CAN YOU HEAR ME NOW?:** Colts communications technician Shannon Almon walks the perimeter of the field inside Reliant Stadium to make sure the wireless signals work inside the helmets of Colts quarterbacks Peyton Manning and Jim Sorgi two hours prior to the start of the game. **Matt Detrich** / The Star

Dayne rushed 32 times for a career-high 153 yards and two touchdowns. If there was a play that typified Dayne's day, it was a third-quarter third-and-8 at the Houston 7-yard line. Dayne bashed up the middle, ran through linebacker Cato June's arm tackle, plunged into the pile and came out the other end for 17 yards and a first down.

"I'd say this is one of the bigger disappointments we've had since I've been here," said Tony Dungy, who is in his fifth season as Colts coach. "You find out about people; you find out about how they bounce back from disappointments."

It went bad from the start.

The Colts were down 14-0 after running only two offensive plays. The Texans drove 61 yards on the game's first series to go up 7-0. After a Peyton Manning incompletion and running back Dominic Rhodes' fumble, Houston was in possession again, on its way to Dayne's second touchdown.

Houston's five scoring drives consisted of 10, nine, 14, 15 and six plays. The last of those was abbreviated only by the clock; the Texans called timeout on second down and kicked the winning field goal.

The Colts had a meager seven possessions, one a single-play kneel-down at the

▲ **HOLIDAY HEADGEAR:** Colts fan Dan Brewer, Austin, Texas, shows his Christmas spirit with a Colts Santa-style hat before the game. Matt Detrich / The Star

▲ **FRAMED:** Colts fan Haylee Koonce, Hungermord, Texas, takes a photo of the Colts players at the start of the game. Matt Kryger / The Star

▶ **MAYBE SHE'LL GET THE TEETH:** Colts fans Amanda Hilliard (left) and her daughter Kassidy Mitchell, 6, both of Lake Charles, La., share a laugh before the start of the game. Matt Detrich / The Star

end of the first half. They scored on four of them.

The Colts had everything to play for, yet it was the Texans who looked the part. Houston played with a spirit and efficiency that made it a shame so many of the 70,132 tickets sold were not used.

"It was buzzing in the huddle," said Houston quarterback David Carr, who was workmanlike in completing 16-of-23 passes for 163 yards and one touchdown.

Only one huddle was buzzing.

"We just didn't play as hard and as well as you need to play to win a game on the road," Dungy said.

No one offered an excuse. There were none. ■

KRAVITZ ON THE COLTS

Time after time, Peyton Manning stood up from his seat on the Indianapolis Colts' bench, stretched his quads, did some toe touches, scraped the turf from his cleats in preparation for battle. It was third down for the Houston Texans, third down again and again and again, and Manning was standing up to prepare himself for that oh-so-rare moment that never seemed to come Sunday — a third-down stop by the Colts' joke of a defense.

And when the game ended with Houston place-kicker Kris Brown's 48-yard field goal carrying between the uprights, there was Manning again, standing silently on the sidelines, his lips pursed, his hands on his hips, haplessly watching the close of another chapter in the Colts' late-season collapse.

▲ **NO ESCAPE:** Colts running back Joseph Addai (29) is tackled by the Texans' Mario Williams in the first quarter. Matt Kryger / The Star

▲ **TAKEDOWN:** Colts linebacker Gary Brackett (58) tackles the Texans' Ron Dayne in the second quarter. Matt Kryger / The Star

◄ **NICE CATCH:** Colts wide receiver Marvin Harrison celebrates his touchdown in the first quarter. Matt Kryger / The Star

▲ **DISCUSSION:** Colts quarterback Peyton Manning listens in as the officials discuss a penalty in the third quarter. Matt Kryger / The Star

▶ **NOT LOOKING GOOD:** Colts coach Tony Dungy glances up at the scoreboard after his team fell behind by two touchdowns in the first quarter. Matt Kryger / The Star

▼ **OPPORTUNITY MISSED:** Peyton Manning falls to the ground while throwing an incomplete pass and failing to get a first down in the third quarter. Matt Kryger / The Star

▲ **GOOD CATCH:** Marvin Harrison catches a touchdown pass in front of the Texans' Demarcus Faggins (38) in the fourth quarter. Matt Kryger / The Star

▲ **FRUSTRATION:** Peyton Manning pounds his fist into the turf after failing to get a first down in the third quarter. Matt Kryger / The Star

Dungy, Colts try to put loss behind them

By Phillip B. Wilson

Tony Dungy's Christmas was spent trying to block out "one of the bigger disappointments" in a five-year run as Indianapolis Colts coach.

"You have to try to do that," the perplexed coach said a day after the Colts lost 27-24 at Houston to slip to a third seed in the AFC playoff picture. "It's tough, but you have to try."

The Colts, who started 9-0, have had four road losses in six games. The Colts' NFL-worst run defense is on the verge of allowing 100 yards rushing in every game for the first time since 1978.

Dungy restated that shoddy tackling and failing to fill the gaps can be fixed when practice resumes , but conceded it's been difficult putting a finger on the inconsistency.

"We've lost three of the games in the fourth quarter and one we just didn't play well. Those are games you have to win to be a champion."

Especially against the Texans (5-10). Ron Dayne ran for a career-high 153

▲ **TROUBLED:** Colts coach Tony Dungy takes a moment to himself in the third quarter. Matt Detrich / The Star

yards. Houston had the ball for 35 minutes, 59 seconds. The Colts' Peyton Manning took a season-low 45 snaps.

Some question if Dungy and his cover-2 scheme of undersized, speedy defenders is the problem. Critics wonder if what was said about him in Tampa Bay is true, that his even-keel approach can't inspire a team to get to the Super Bowl. Jon Gruden took over the Bucs in 2002 and won the title the next season.

"It's been that way my whole career and probably will continue to be that way," he said of the knock. "We've just got to win more often than we lose."

▲ **CONGRATS:** Colts place-kicker Adam Vinatieri (left) congratulates Texans kicker Kris Brown after he made a 48-yard field goal to defeat the Colts 27-24. **Matt Kryger** / The Star

◄ **SCOREBOARD WATCHING:** Colts running backs Joseph Addai (left) and Dominic Rhodes, who had a fumble in the first quarter, watch the screen moments before the field goal beat the Colts. **Matt Detrich** / The Star

◄◄ **HE CAN'T LOOK:** Colts defensive back Marlin Jackson can't stand to watch the field goal attempt that beat the Colts on the game's final play. **Matt Detrich** / The Star

A LITTLE MO' TO GO

Colts hold off Dolphins, enter playoffs with some momentum

By Phil Richards

Coach Tony Dungy told his Indianapolis Colts to play Sunday like the playoffs already had begun. It was a good thing they did.

The Colts' 27-22 victory over the Miami Dolphins went down to the final snap. It had the drama if not the finality of a playoff game and it kept the sellout RCA Dome crowd of 57,310 alternating between their feet and the edge of their seats right to the end.

The Colts closed the regular season with an 8-0 home record and they will be right back at work at the RCA Dome at 4:30 p.m. Saturday. As the AFC's No. 3 playoff seed, the Colts (12-4) will open the postseason with a wild-card game against the sixth-seeded Kansas City Chiefs (9-7).

"We're happy to get out of it with a win and now I think

◄ **HARD YARDAGE:** The Colts' Joseph Addai tries for third-quarter yardage against the Dolphins. Sam Riche / The Star

▶ **TROT ON IN:** Colts wide receiver Marvin Harrison hauls in this fourth-quarter pass for a touchdown. Sam Riche / The Star

NFL Week Seventeen

Colts 27
Dolphins 22

Team record: 12-4

everybody's back to 0-0," said Dungy. "I told the rookies in the locker room that everything's completely different now. The stakes get a little higher."

The Colts had lost three of their previous four games and four of their past six, all on the road. They desperately needed to win, and just about everyone lent a hand.

The offense scored 10 points in the span of 19 seconds during the final minute of the first half.

Backup wide receiver Aaron Moorehead made a career-long 36-yard catch to set up a touchdown.

Dan Klecko, a 275-pound defensive tackle, scored one. Klecko was inserted at fullback and scored his first NFL touchdown on a 2-yard pass from quarterback Peyton Manning.

"It's all about winning now," said linebacker Cato June, whose interception was central to the 10-point burst. "No matter

how you get it done, no matter who does it, win."

The Dolphins (6-10) were taking the last steps of a lost season. Cleo Lemon, their No. 3 quarterback, was making his first start. Running back Ronnie Brown was playing his second game since returning from three games on the sideline with a broken left hand.

No matter. It was a fight right down to the last play, when Colts end Robert

▲ FINISHING TOUCHES: Staying dry and painting faces in the back of their SUV outside the RCA Dome are (left to right) Sarah Campbell, Raleigh, N.C.; Amanda Green, Evansville, Ind.; and Erica Klueh, Vincennes, Ind. **Sam Riche** / The Star

◄ FANATICAL: The Four Horseman, led by Jake Berry (right) walk around the RCA Dome cheering on fans before the game.
Matt Kryger / The Star

▶ HAPPY NEW YEAR: Clarke Scott, Alta Vista, Va., rings in the New Year while tailgating before the game. **Sam Riche** / The Star

Mathis flushed Lemon from the pocket and forced him to throw wildly, through the end zone, almost into the stands.

"All out, nothing held back, play to the last play," Mathis said. "That's the way it's going to be in the play-offs."

Manning completed 22-of-37 passes for 282 yards and two touchdowns with no interceptions. Working against the NFL's No. 3-rated defense, he and his teammates had to find their opportunities where they could, and exploit them.

The Colts squeezed a lot of football into the final 1½ minutes of the first half.

Starting at the Indianapolis 20, Manning completed 4-of-6 passes for 69 yards, the big one a 36-yarder to Moorehead that carried to the Miami 11.

Manning dropped to pass again. Dolphins linebacker Zach Thomas blitzed. Manning scrambled left.

▲ **LOOKING FOR YARDS:** Marvin Harrison heads upfield after a first-half catch. Sam Riche / The Star

◀ **ANTICIPATION:** Mark Maldeney (from the left), Troy Mynhier, Angie Mynhier and Missy Maldeney take in the view from an upper concourse window that looks out on the under-construction Lucas Oil Stadium. "We can't wait," Mark Maldeney said of the completion of the project.
Robert Scheer / The Star

◀◀ **BELIEVERS:** Colts fans (from the left) Doug Gehring, Dana Gehring, Mandi Kemerly and Shane Kemerly, all from Lapel, Ind., cheer on the Colts at the start of the game. Matt Kryger / The Star

HE'S A NATURAL: Defensive tackle Dan Klecko (left) scores the first touchdown for the Colts as he gets past Dolphins cornerback Will Allen. *Sam Riche / The Star*

CROSSING THE LINE: The Colts' Dan Klecko scores on a touchdown pass in first-quarter action. *Sam Riche / The Star*

Miami end Jason Taylor chased. Manning dug hard. He dropped his shoulder and blasted through safeties Jason Allen and Renaldo Hill at the goal line.

Big hit. Big play. Touchdown.

Center Jeff Saturday was so excited he got face mask to face mask with his quarterback and screamed. The crowd roared, too.

"A little smash-mouth football from the quarterback," Saturday said. "I was extremely excited. When you get the opportunity to make something special happen, you've got to be the guy to do it.

"I think we had a lot of guys do that today and that's what the playoffs are all about."

The Colts had covered 80 yards in 1:12. Only 19 seconds remained, but the home

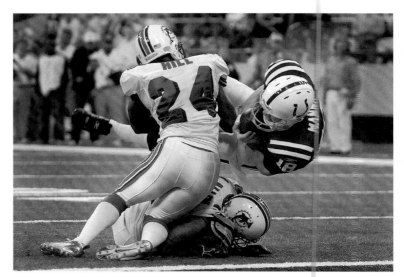

▲ **TOUGH CROWD:** A Colts fan shares her feelings about the person she is with at the game. **Matt Kryger** / The Star

◀ **ON THE RUN:** Peyton Manning scrambles by the Dolphins' Jason Taylor on an 11-yard touchdown run in the second quarter. **Matt Kryger** / The Star

▲ **HARD HITTING:** Colts quarterback Peyton Manning dives for a touchdown as he is hit by the Dolphins' Jason Allen (bottom) and Renaldo Hill (24) in the second quarter. **Matt Kryger** / The Star

▲ **KEEP MOVING:** Indianapolis Colts tight end Bryan Fletcher tries to break free on this first-half pass play. **Sam Riche** / The Star

▶ **GOOD KICK:** The Colts' Adam Vinatieri hits this field goal during the third quarter. **Sam Riche** / The Star

team wasn't finished.

On Miami's first play after the kickoff, June slashed in front of wide receiver Wes Welker and intercepted Lemon's pass. June returned the football 8 yards to the Miami 37 with six seconds to play.

Joseph Addai ran for 9 yards, and had the presence of mind to get down and call timeout with the clock reading 0:02. Adam Vinatieri's 46-yard field goal attempt was true.

Ten points in 19 seconds.

It was 17-6. It was crazy. It will stay that way. It's playoff time. ■

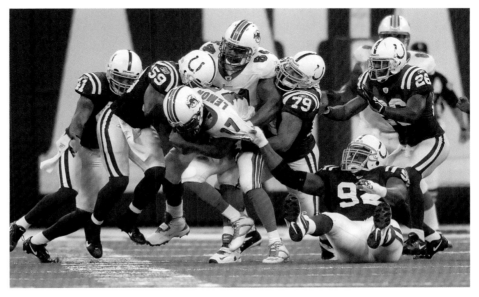

◀ **SACKED:** Colts Cato June (59), Raheem Brock (79) and Anthony McFarland (92) sack Dolphins quarterback Cleo Lemon (17) in the third quarter. **Matt Kryger** / The Star

◀◀ **UP FOR GRABS:** Colts linebacker Cato June (center) holds on to an interception near the end of the second quarter, as Miami players Wes Welker (left) and Randy McMichael try to bring him down. **Robert Scheer** / The Star

▶GOOD GRAB: Colts tight end Dallas Clark (44) makes a one-handed catch in front of the Dolphins' Zach Thomas in the fourth quarter.

Matt Kryger / The Star

▲DUCK AND COVER: The Colts' Anthony McFarland (92) hammers Dolphins quarterback Cleo Lemon in second-half action.

Sam Riche / The Star

▶DIVING FOR IT: Colts defensive back Jason David looks to pick off this Miami pass during the fourth quarter. He couldn't get a hand on it.

Robert Scheer / The Star

▶▶FRIENDLY RIVALRY: Colts coach Tony Dungy (right) greets Dolphins coach Nick Saban following the game.

Matt Kryger / The Star

BOB KRAVITZ'S REPORT CARD

C- **RUN OFFENSE:** Of course, when you're talking about the Colts' running game, the conversation begins and ends with their fleet quarterback, Peyton Manning. When somebody mentioned he threw 31 touchdown passes and had just nine interceptions, which is remarkable, by the way, Manning added, "And four rushing touchdowns." It's not often a Manning run/gallop/scamper rates as a game-changing play. In a perfect world, he wouldn't have to lower his head and take on three Dolphins to reach the end zone, but when you're a running quarterback, you do these things.

B **PASS OFFENSE:** In the same general vein, when you think about the Colts' high-powered pass offense, your thoughts inevitably turn to Dan Klecko, son of Joe Klecko, of the Pass Catching Kleckos. Nice to see Dallas Clark back, too. The rust showed a few times, then he made that diving grab over the middle that shows why his presence is required if the Colts are going to make a postseason run. By the way, if this was Dolphins defensive end Jason Taylor's last game — he was talking retirement after the game — then that's too bad. He might not be a sure Hall of Famer, but he is a good one, and I loved the way he lit up San Diego's Shawne Merriman last week.

B- **RUN DEFENSE:** OK, I know what you're saying: Kravitz is already into the champagne on New Year's Eve. A B- grade? Listen up, we're grading on a Colts curve. They gave up 150 yards rushing. That's 24 fewer than their average. So the 5.8-yard average was fairly abysmal, but still, the total wasn't bad and they generally kept the Dolphins out of the end zone. It's always good to keep expectations minimal. That's how my wife has managed to stay married to me all these years.

B **PASS DEFENSE:** It occurred to me in the third quarter that nobody complains anymore about Nick Harper and Jason David. That either means that Harper and David had one heck of a good regular season, or the run defense is so bad, the corners don't get any action and we have absolutely no idea either way. By the way, if you blinked, you missed the Cleo Lemon Era. In the interest of continuing these non sequiturs, it should be noted Bob Sanders reported he is healthy and will play Saturday.

D **SPECIAL TEAMS:** Every week, we talk about how the Colts' run defense is going to get them beaten in the playoffs and, while that might be the case, I'm putting even money on Indy's kick return team. Let it be said, Mike Vanderjagt has been exonerated as the reason the Colts' kick return coverage was so lousy for all those years. Even with Adam Vinatieri on hand, they're still last in the league in kick coverage. After the game, coach Tony Dungy said there will be personnel changes. I'm thinking, save yourself the trouble and just kick it out of bounds.

B **COACHING:** Forget about this game, which shouldn't be that difficult to do. The ultimate coaching litmus test for Dungy and Co. comes now. They've come into the playoffs as heavy favorites before and fizzled. This time, they are properly viewed as vulnerable long shots. After five years, can Dungy and his staff produce a long postseason run when nobody is looking? Four years of 12-plus victories is awfully impressive and shouldn't be dismissed, but Dungy was brought here to lead the Colts to the Super Bowl. The grades the next few weeks (or maybe just next week) are the ones that matter.

B- **INTANGIBLES:** Two weeks ago against Cincinnati, the Colts played like their hair was on fire. One week later, they flat-lined in Houston and produced what Dungy called the most disappointing regular-season performance of his time here. The effort against the Dolphins fell somewhere in between. All things considered, you'd rather they were playing at the top of their game heading into the playoffs. But, then, 20 teams are packing up and making tee times, so at least they have an opportunity, which is something. (P.S. Can Hunter Smith come back for the playoffs? Please?)

DAY OF THE DEFENSE

Believe it: Colts deliver record showing

By Phil Richards

With little more than a minute to play Saturday at the RCA Dome, one of the quietest Colts put on a show. After containing Kansas City for 59 minutes there was no containing the joy.

Rookie safety Antoine Bethea intercepted a Trent Green pass, stepped out of bounds at the Chiefs 36, then in celebration dashed down the sideline and into the end zone. He was joined there by a half-dozen teammates in a victory dance that got the sell-out crowd of 57,215 rocking.

"Everybody swarmed the ball. Everybody had fun," Bethea gushed after the Indianapolis

Wild-Card Game

Colts 23
Chiefs 8

Team record: 13-4

◀ **BLUE WAVE:** Colts defenders (from the left) Gary Brackett, Marlin Jackson, Anthony McFarland and Robert Mathis swarm Chiefs running back Larry Johnson. The Indianapolis defense, ranked 32nd against the run, held the NFL's No. 2 rusher to 32 yards on 13 carries.
Matt Detrich / The Star

▶ **THAT'S WHAT I LIKE:** Dwight Freeney celebrates after sacking Trent Green in the first half. **Sam Riche** / The Star

Colts' 23-8 AFC wild-card playoff victory. "We've been like robots out there and today we were just out there playing and enjoying ourselves."

The victory earned the Colts (13-4) a divisional-round date at Baltimore (13-3) next Saturday.

A Colts' run defense that ranked 32nd in the NFL played championship defense Saturday. It didn't play like robots. It played with passion and purpose. It smothered Chiefs running back Larry Johnson. It battered Green. It picked up the Colts' struggling offense and carried it.

The numbers were stunning. Johnson, who rushed for 1,789 yards during the regular season, ran 13 times for 32 yards against the Colts. Kansas City (9-8) ran for 44 yards, 129 fewer than the Colts' average yield this season and a franchise post-season record. The Chiefs totaled 126 net yards, another Colts playoff record.

"Defense. Defense. Defense," the crowd chanted. Replays of big hits and big plays drew roars.

▲ PREGAME HOSTILITIES: Colts fan Andy Diruzza (left) and Chiefs fan Pat Swindell, both from Alexandria, Ind., lock horns while tailgating before the game. **Matt Kryger** / The Star

▲ TOUCH-UP PAINT: Colts fan Kenny Bogle, Danville, Ind., touches up the paint job on his face while tailgating. **Matt Kryger** / The Star

◄ LET'S GO: Colts quarterback Peyton Manning slaps hands with his teammates as the starters are introduced before the AFC wild-card playoff game against the Chiefs. **Matt Detrich** / The Star

There were plenty. The Colts were fed up.

"We've got the worst defense ever. The worst defense that's ever been assembled," linebacker Cato June snorted. "This was about 11 guys just stepping up and doing it. It wasn't about changing this or that. It was you beat your man and just do it."

The defense did it.

With the offense spinning its wheels and settling for field goals for most of three quarters, the defense saved the day.

Colts quarterback Peyton Manning threw three interceptions. The Colts were 0-11 when Manning threw three or more interceptions. That's 0-10 during the regular season and 0-1 in the playoffs.

Not Saturday.

"All the people out there saying our quarterback has to be perfect and all that, uh, uh," nose tackle Anthony "Booger" McFarland said. "This game is bigger than one person."

◀ **GOOD COVERAGE:** Chiefs wide receiver Eddie Kennison (87) has the ball knocked out of his hands by Colts defensive back Nick Harper in the first quarter. **Matt Detrich** / The Star

▲ **IS THAT ALL YOU GOT?:** Colts tight end Dallas Clark (right) survives a flying tackle from Chiefs linebacker Kawika Mitchell in the first quarter. **Matt Detrich** / The Star

◀ **ONE AND COUNTING:** Colts place-kicker Adam Vinatieri kicks the first of two field goals in the first quarter. **Sam Riche** / The Star

The defense was an 11-man band for all 60 minutes.

On the first play from scrimmage, Johnson blasted into the middle. Colts tackle Raheem Brock and end Robert Mathis blasted into Johnson. No gain.

On second down, Johnson smashed off left guard. Cornerback Nick Harper smashed into Johnson. A 2-yard gain.

So it went.

The Colts defense had produced seven three-and-outs in its past seven games. It produced five in the first half Saturday. The Chiefs ran four plays on their only other first-half possession, then

◀◀IT'S GOOD: Colts fans cheer as Adam Vinatieri (4) kicks his second field goal in the first quarter. **Robert Scheer** / The Star

◀YES!: Colts safety Matt Giordano reacts after a big hit in the first half. **Sam Riche** / The Star

▲ FUTILE EFFORT: Peyton Manning (18) tries in vain to bring down Kansas City cornerback Ty Law in the second quarter. Law had intercepted a Manning pass and returned it 43 yards before being tackled by Marvin Harrison. **Robert Scheer** / The Star

◀NOT TODAY: Colts defensive back Marlin Jackson (right) brings down Chiefs running back Larry Johnson. The Colts limited Johnson, who was the NFL's second-leading rusher during the regular season, to an average of 2.5 yards per carry. His longest run was 6 yards. **Sam Riche** / The Star

▲ **NICE PICKUP:** The Colts' Marvin Harrison snags a first-quarter pass for a big gain. **Sam Riche** / The Star

▲ **PERFECT!:** Adam Vinatieri reacts after going 3-for-3 on field goals. **Matt Detrich** / The Star

▼ **GOOD CATCH:** Dallas Clark goes down after a catch against the Chiefs' Greg Wesley (25). **Sam Riche** / The Star

place-kicker Lawrence Tynes boinked a 23-yard field goal attempt off the left upright.

By halftime, the Colts had run up a total yardage advantage of 255-16. Utter domination produced a 9-0 lead.

The defense just kept playing.

It yielded one drive, an 8-play, 60-yard maneuver that cut the Colts' lead to 16-8. That was that.

Playing only his third game in almost four months, safety Bob Sanders intercepted a Green pass on the next series.

When Colts punter Hunter Smith dropped a snap, Kansas City threatened at the Colts 37. Three times in

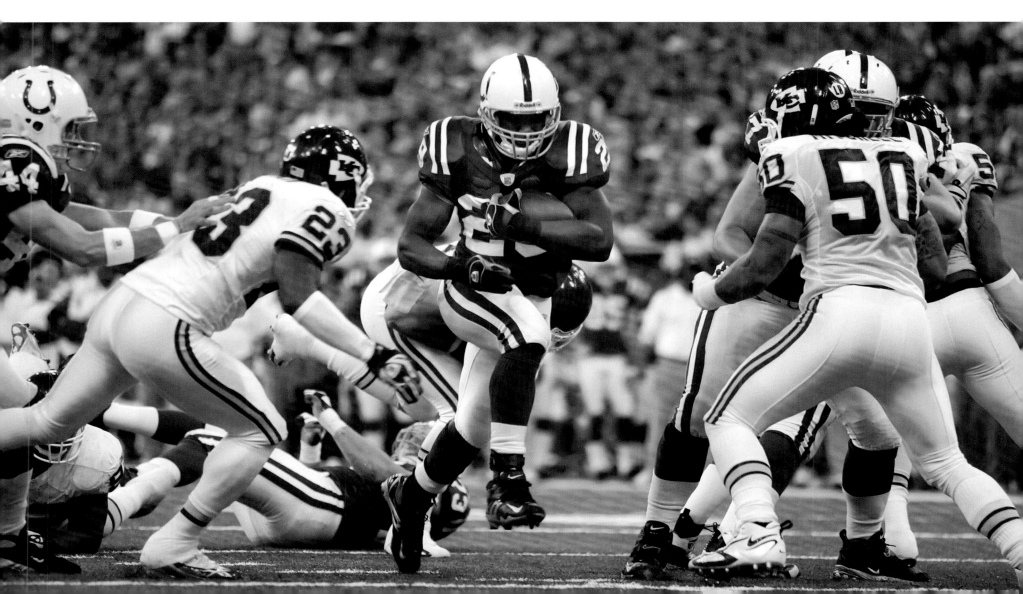

▼ **NOW THAT'S A HOLE:** Colts running back Joseph Addai runs through a huge hole created by the offensive line's blocks and heads into the secondary. Addai averaged 4.9 yards on his 25 carries. **Sam Riche** / The Star

a five-play sequence, the Colts sacked Green. End Dwight Freeney got him. McFarland got him. Then Mathis and end Bo Schobel hit him again. The football popped loose. Colts lineman Josh Thomas recovered.

Next series, next big play: Bethea's interception. It was dance fever.

"All the stats and all that stuff during the season doesn't matter in the playoffs," said Freeney, who had two sacks and forced a fumble. "It's playoff time."

The numbers say the league's best defense resides in Baltimore and awaits the Colts. What happened Saturday at the Dome suggested something very different, at least for a day.

Whew. What a day.

"The playoffs are about winning or going home," linebacker Gary Brackett said. "Me personally, I'm not packed. I'm not planning on going anywhere." ■

◀ **SEALING THE DEAL:** Colts wide receiver Reggie Wayne (87) pulls in a touchdown pass over Chiefs defenders Patrick Surtain (23) and Greg Wesley in the fourth quarter. That touchdown gave the Colts a 23-8 lead. **Matt Detrich** / The Star

▲ **CELEBRATION:** Reggie Wayne celebrates his touchdown catch with teammate Tarik Glenn in the fourth quarter. **Sam Riche** / The Star

▼ **BRINGING THE PRESSURE:** Colts defenders Dwight Freeney and Raheem Brock sack Chiefs quarterback Trent Green late in the game. The Colts sacked Green four times, three of them coming late in the fourth quarter. **Sam Riche** / The Star

▶ **GOING DOWN AGAIN:** Anthony McFarland (92) closes in on Trent Green for this fourth-quarter sack. **Robert Scheer** / The Star

▶▶ **WRAPPING IT UP:** Colts defensive end Robert Mathis (98) celebrates a sack on Trent Green late in the fourth quarter. **Matt Detrich** / The Star

▲ **CAN'T STOP SMILING:** Antoine Bethea (41) and teammate Cato June celebrate Bethea's late game interception. **Sam Riche** / The Star

BOB KRAVITZ'S REPORT CARD

A– **RUN OFFENSE:** Since we spend so much time in this space singing the praises of Joseph Addai and wondering why Dominic Rhodes starts or gets quite so many carries, let it be mentioned, Rhodes was terrific Saturday. The offensive line was dominant, especially slowing down Kansas City's two active defensive ends. The Colts still need to be better in short-yardage situations — have to score with second-and-goal at the 2, right? — but it's nitpicking.

B **PASS OFFENSE:** You know it's not a normal game when we're writing that Peyton Manning did a good job of managing the game. Or that he was smart to just hand off or dink the ball five yards underneath to Dallas Clark and Addai. For a while there, I'll be honest, I was thinking it was time to write the Peyton-as-Alex-Rodriguez column. Let's just say, he didn't exactly dispel the notion that he's not a playoff quarterback. Is Ty Law in his head? He's rented a condo in Peyton's cerebral cortex. Manning's got to bring the laser rocket arm to Baltimore, or else.

A+ **RUN DEFENSE:** Thirty two yards. Larry Johnson had 32 rushing yards. The defensive line dominated a strong Chiefs line. The linebackers wrapped up, didn't miss a tackle. The secondary was as strong against the run as it's been all season. It was like watching football in a parallel universe. Who were those guys, and who let them out to play in the postseason? It's hard to know where to start, or with whom. Booger was great. Freeney was great. Marlin Jackson was great. Etc., etc.

A **PASS DEFENSE:** Maybe my stat crew can check this one: It seemed like the Colts "D" forced more three-and-outs in one game than they did all season. Wait. I don't have a stat crew. No room in the budget. Anyway, the pass rush was vicious, relentless and lots of other words that don't come immediately to mind. The folks in Kansas City will wonder why Trent Green didn't get the hook, but the way that group played Saturday, would another quarterback have made that much difference?

B+ **SPECIAL TEAMS:** OK, so Hunter Smith flubbed a punt snap (he's still bummed about Notre Dame's Sugar Bowl performance). And Adam Vinatieri, who was generally impeccable in every other way, kicked one out of bounds. Other than that, Vinatieri kept showing why he's the best big-game kicker ever and the kick-return team, facing the dangerous Dante Hall, was flawless. It makes you wonder, if the Colts' best athletes were on the kick coverage team during the regular season, might they have beaten Houston and held onto the second seed?

A– **COACHING:** Here's hoping Tony Dungy isn't real close with Brian Billick, because, quite frankly, I've had enough friendship for one postseason. According to the folks on the TV broadcast, Dungy went to dinner Friday night with Herm Edwards. No problem there, but remember when Jermaine O'Neal socialized before the playoffs with Rasheed Wallace, or Terrell Owens went to the Eagles' hotel in Dallas and played dominoes with his old mates? I just ask these kinds of questions to keep myself entertained.

A– **INTANGIBLES:** This would seem to be as good a time as any to bring up my favorite statistic, the quarterback rating. Did you realize that Hunter Smith, whose Yepremian-esque effort to Rocky Boiman left him 1-for-1 passing for minus-16 yards, had a quarterback rating of 79.2, which was higher than Manning? You see that, you marvel at just how awful Rex Grossman had to be to put up a 1.2 a couple of weeks back. Quick thought: I've got to see about renting a Mayflower moving van for the trip to Baltimore. Just for fun.

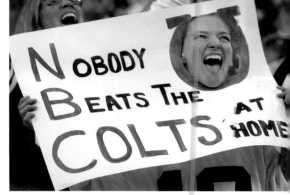

▲ **JUBILATION:** Colts fan Valerie Thomas Noblesville, Ind., celebrates the Colts' victory. Matt Kryger / The Star

◄ **SATISFACTION:** The Colts' Joseph Addai is all smiles leaving the field after rushing for 122 yards against the Chiefs. Sam Riche / The Star

▼ **DIFFERENCE MAKER:** Colts safety Bob Sanders celebrates the win with fans as he leaves the field. Sanders had been injured for most of the year, but shored up the Colts defense against the Chiefs. Sam Riche / The Star

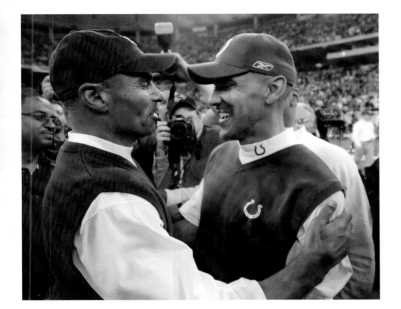

◀ **STILL FRIENDS:** Colts coach Tony Dungy (right) hugs his friend Kansas City Chiefs coach Herm Edwards following the game. **Matt Kryger** / The Star

▼ **LOOK WHO'S TALKING NOW:** Colts defensive tackle Anthony McFarland reacts to the win.

Sam Riche / The Star

COLSPLAYOFFS

WILD-CARD GAME
COLTS 23, CHIEFS 8

Day of the defense

BELIEVE IT: COLTS DELIVER RECORD SHOWING

BY THE NUMBERS, BIZARRO EDITION

32
Larry Johnson's rushing yards. Wasn't he supposed to run right through this Colts defense? Didn't he gain 1,789 in the regular season?

44
Total rushing yards allowed by the Colts. That's a franchise postseason record, 64 fewer than their previous low this season and 129 under their league-worst average.

0
Chiefs first downs in the first half. The last time a team managed that in a playoff game was 1960. K.C. got its first with 3½ minutes left in the third quarter and finished with seven.

16
Total yards for the Chiefs in the first half. The Colts had 255.

3
Interceptions for Peyton Manning. Isn't that supposed to spell doom for the Colts? It had the previous 11 times he'd done it.

OFFENSIVE AWARDS GO TO:

The rookie . . .
Running back Joseph Addai made the first start of his career and he was up to the assignment. Addai ran 25 times for 122 yards and a touchdown to become the sixth Colts back to rush for 100 yards in the playoffs. The only other rookie to do it was Zack Crockett, who ran for 147 yards during a 1995 wild-card victory at San Diego.

. . . and the kicker
Adam Vinatieri went 3-for-3, converting field goals of 48, 39 and 50 yards. He is 26-for-26 at the RCA Dome, and he tied Tony Fritsch's NFL record by kicking a field goal in his 13th consecutive postseason game.

BLUE WAVE: Colts defenders (from left) Gary Brackett, Marlin Jackson, Anthony McFarland and Robert Mathis swarm after Chiefs running back Larry Johnson. The Indianapolis defense, ranked 32nd against the run, held the NFL's No. 2 rusher to 32 yards on 13 carries. "This was about 11 guys just stepping up and doing it," linebacker Cato June said.

MATT DETRICH / The Star

FRESH LEGS: Colts rookie Joseph Addai picks up yards in the third quarter. In his first start, he rushed for 122 yards and one TD on 25 carries.

ROBERT SCHEER / The Star

PERFECT: Adam Vinatieri reacts after going 3-for-3 on field goals.

AND NOW: THE RAVENS

Next up is a trip to Baltimore for an AFC divisional-round game at 4:30 p.m. Saturday. The second-seeded Ravens (13-3) have won nine of their past 10 games, have the league's No. 1 defense yardage-wise and also have allowed a league-low 12.6 points a game.

▶▶ **For a closer look at the Ravens, see page P2.**

Defense, Addai help pick up struggling Manning; Ravens next

By Phil Richards
phil.richards@indystar.com

With little more than a minute to play Saturday at the RCA Dome, one of the quietest Colts put on a show. After containing Kansas City for 59 minutes there was no containing the joy.

Rookie safety Antoine Bethea intercepted a Trent Green pass, stepped out of bounds at the Chiefs 36, then in celebration dashed down the sideline into the end zone. He was joined there by a half-dozen teammates in a victory dance that got the sell-out crowd of 57,215 rocking.

"Everybody swarmed the ball.

Everybody had fun," Bethea gushed after the Indianapolis Colts' 23-8 AFC wild-card playoff victory. "We've been like robots out there and today we were just out there playing and enjoying ourselves."

The victory earned the Colts (13-4) a divisional-round date at Baltimore (13-3) next Saturday at 4:30 p.m.

A Colts' run defense that ranked 32nd in the NFL played championship defense Saturday. It didn't play like robots. It played with passion and purpose. It smothered Chiefs running back Larry Johnson. It bat-

tered Green. It picked up the Colts' struggling offense and carried it.

The numbers were stunning. Johnson, who rushed for 1,789 yards during the regular season, ran 13 times for 32 yards against the Colts. Kansas City (9-8) ran for 44 yards, 120 fewer than the Colts' average yield this season and a franchise postseason record. The Chiefs totaled 126 net yards, another Colts playoff record.

"Defense. Defense. Defense," the crowd chanted. Replays of

See Colts, Page P6

See Colts, Page P6

Sure, we knew all along this Colts defense could do it

O h, there was some yapping going on in the Indianapolis Colts' postgame locker room Saturday. Mostly good-natured yapping, it should be noted, but yapping nonetheless. And how could you begrudge The Worst Defense Ever for beating its chest a little bit after 60 minutes of swarming and pursuing and tackling and playing like the 1985 Chicago Bears?

BOB KRAVITZ

Let the yapping commence.
"We have the worst run defense that's ever been assembled,"

Cato June said facetiously as the media gathered around his locker. "Just rip us. Say we're too little and too fast to play these great running backs. We like the negativity. We feed off it. We're going to allow you guys to tell us what we can't do next week. Next week, everybody will say, 'Oh, (Baltimore's) Jamal Lewis is 250 pounds and you're 210, how are you going to stop him?'"

June shrugged.
When somebody innocently

wondered, where's that been all year, June laughed, then tried to maintain a straight face.

"You know, we were purposely sand-bagging," June said mischievously. "We wanted everybody to say we had the worst defense ever. It was just a sandbag technique."

Well done, wouldn't you say? Seriously, most people would look at Jacksonville's 375-yard rushing effort and think, "You know, the Colts aren't very good against the

run." But now the truth can be told: It was all a ruse. It was football's answer to the rope-a-dope. Genius, if you ask me. Absolute genius.

Yep, they were yapping. And it hardly seemed polite to remind them that two weeks after they dominated the Philadelphia Eagles, they got trashed by Jacksonville. Or the fact that after they lit up Cincinnati on a Mon-

See Kravitz, Page P6

See Kravitz, Page P6

Manning stays cool, finishes strong
Colts quarterback **Peyton Manning** threw three interceptions but righted himself late to lead two TD drives. **P4**

Addai runs for triple digits
Colts rookie **Joseph Addai**, in his first NFL start, goes for 122 rushing yards and joins an elite group. **P5**

Cowboys let win get away
Tony Romo botches the hold on a game-winning field goal and the Seahawks edge the Cowboys 21-20. **P7**

SOMETHING SPECIAL AFOOT
Vinatieri hits 5 field goals

By Mike Chappell

BALTIMORE — Closure will have to wait for a city spurned. So will the offseason for the Indianapolis Colts.

Emotions were raw and anger palpable Saturday evening at M&T Bank Stadium as the Colts made their first playoff appearance here since relocating to Indianapolis in 1984. But the largest crowd ever to see a game here — 71,162 — wandered into the cool night air disappointed, with their beloved Baltimore Ravens behind them.

The Colts? They're movin' on to next Sunday's AFC Championship Game for the third time since 1995 after riding Adam Vinatieri's five field goals and a suddenly-stiff defense to a 15-6 victory over the Ravens in a divisional matchup. The Colts will either host New England, should the Patriots upset

AFC Divisional Game

Colts 15
Ravens 6

Team record: 14-4

◄ **THAT'LL DO IT:** Colts defensive tackle Anthony McFarland (92) and the rest of the team celebrate the last field goal by Adam Vinatieri to seal the 15-6 victory in the AFC divisional playoff game at M&T Bank Stadium in Baltimore.
Matt Detrich / The Star

▶ **IS IT GOOD?:** Adam Vinatieri (4) connects on his fourth of five field goals in the game. This 48-yard boot gave the Colts a 12-3 lead in the third quarter.
Matt Kryger / The Star

▲**ANTAGONISTIC HATS:** Colts fans Steve Kraabel (left) and his son Hans Kraabel, both from Carmel, Ind., wear Mayflower movers hats that they found online, as they wait at the airport for their flight to see the Colts play the Ravens. Matt Kryger / The Star

▶**FAMILY RIVALRY:** Colts fan Matt Schlessel (right) gets put in a headlock by his mom Joyce Harden, a Ravens fan, before the teams' AFC playoff game. Matt Kryger / The Star

▼**A FRIENDLY FACE:** Colts fan Matt Weir (right), York, Pa., slaps hands with fellow fan Zack Pasley as they meet in a tailgate lot outside M&T Stadium. Many Ravens fans weren't quite so friendly. Matt Detrich / The Star

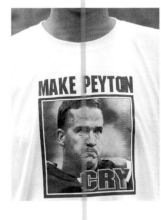

▲**MEAN FANS:** A Baltimore fan shows what he hoped would be in store for Colts quarterback Peyton Manning. Matt Detrich / The Star

◀**TAKE THAT:** Shane Headlee, Brownsburg, Ind., cheers for the Colts. Matt Kryger / The Star

the Chargers, or travel to No. 1 seed San Diego.

For a second straight game, the defense asserted itself. It limited the Ravens to 244 total yards, 2-of-11 on third downs and a pair of Matt Stover field goals. It came up with four takeaways.

"We weren't worried about what was going on, on the outside," defensive tackle Raheem Brock said of the emotion surrounding the game. "We

◄ **THE FIRST OF FIVE:** Adam Vinatieri kicks his first field goal of the day. Sam Riche / The Star

▼ **STRIPPED:** Colts running back Joseph Addai has the ball stripped from his arms by Terrell Suggs of the Ravens in the first quarter. Matt Detrich / The Star

know we can play when we go out there, and that's what we did. We executed."

No one more than Vinatieri. For the umpteenth time, he reaffirmed his reputation as the best clutch kicker in NFL history. His five field goals tied an NFL postseason record. He now has booted 34, eclipsing Gary Anderson's NFL playoff record (32).

Vinatieri's 51-yarder was a personal postseason best and sent the Colts into halftime with a 9-3 lead. His 35-yarder with 23 seconds to play sealed it.

As Vinatieri's final field goal sailed through the uprights, coach Tony Dungy looked on and offered an appropriate postscript.

"Money," he said. "Money."

▲ **ON THE BALL:** Gary Brackett celebrates a fumble recovery in the first quarter. Matt Kryger / The Star

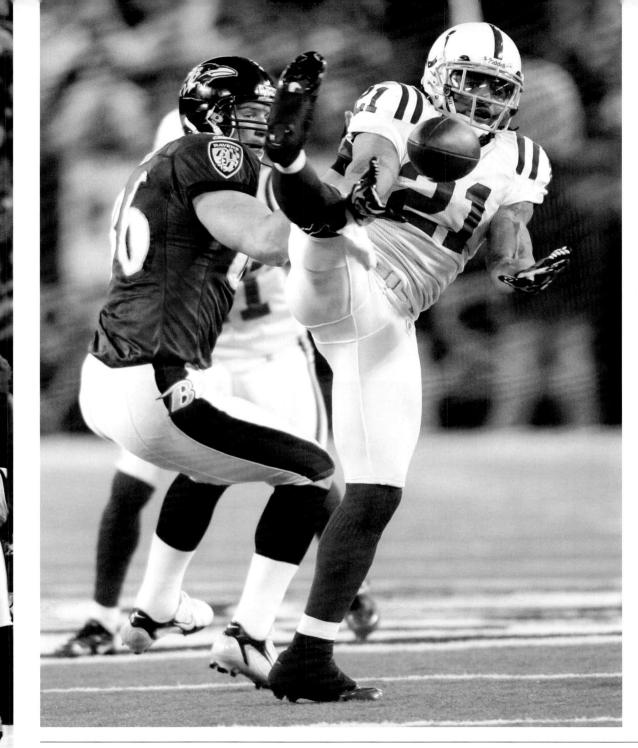

Just another day at the office, insisted Vinatieri, who is 8-for-8 in the postseason and has made his past 15 attempts overall.

"I think you have to go out there and perform every single time you go on the field," he said.

It took the best of Vinatieri and the very best of the defense for the Colts to prevail in such a hostile environment and against such

▲ **WATCH THE BOUNCING BALL:** Marvin Harrison (88) fumbles the ball out of bounds after being tackled by Ravens defensive back Corey Ivy in the third quarter. Matt Kryger / The Star

◄ **SO CLOSE:** Colts safety Bob Sanders (21) nearly intercepts a pass intended for Todd Heap. The Colts had two interceptions and two fumble recoveries. Matt Detrich / The Star

◄◄ **READING THE DEFENSE:** Colts quarterback Peyton Manning (18) calls an audible on the line of scrimmage in the second quarter. Matt Detrich / The Star

▲ **TAKING DOWN THE BIG MAN:** Colts defensive back Antoine Bethea (41) hits Ravens running back Jamal Lewis in the third quarter. **Matt Kryger** / The Star

▼ **KEY FIRST DOWN:** The Colts' Peyton Manning (center) celebrates with his teammates at midfield after the Colts got a first down just before the two-minute warning in the fourth quarter. **Sam Riche** / The Star

▲ **FIVE-FOR-FIVE:** Kicker Adam Vinatieri watches his fifth field goal sail through the uprights with 23 seconds left.

Sam Riche / The Star

◀ **GIMME FIVE:** Adam Vinatieri (4) celebrates with Hunter Smith after he kicked his fifth field goal of the game.

Matt Kryger / The Star

than Dungy found himself hugging defensive tackle Anthony "Booger" McFarland. They recalled their days together in Tampa Bay, when defense ruled.

"(We) were talking at the end of the game," Dungy said. "It was kind of a throwback game for us. We used to win a lot of games this way, so we kind of went back old school on them."

It's called Buc Ball, Colts' style.

Buc Ball?

"Scoring few points," Dungy said, "but winning." ■

◀ **HAPPY GUY:** Colts defensive tackle Anthony McFarland is overcome with emotion as he revels in the Colts' win. **Matt Detrich** / The Star

◀ **COACHES CELEBRATION:** Colts coach Tony Dungy (left) is all smiles as he hugs running backs coach Gene Huey after the Colts' win.
Matt Detrich / The Star

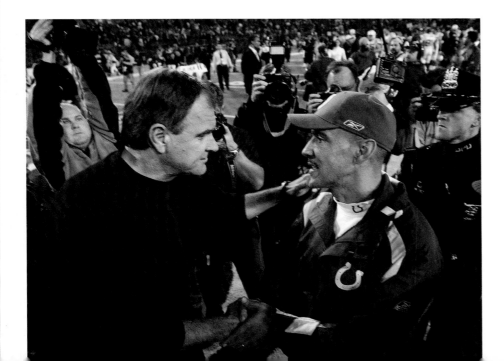

◄◄SMILES ALL AROUND:
Colts tight end Dallas Clark
(right) celebrates the win
with offensive guard Ryan
Lilja (center) as teammate
Dylan Gandy smiles as well.
Matt Detrich / The Star

◄YES!: Kicker Adam
Vinatieri celebrates the win
as he leaves the field.
Sam Riche / The Star

▼ COACHES' MEETING:
Colts coach Tony Dungy
meets Ravens coach Brian
Billick at midfield after
the Colts' win.
Sam Riche / The Star

BOB KRAVITZ'S
REPORT CARD

B **RUN OFFENSE:** Hey, you know what I liked the most about the running game? The fact the Colts kept running the ball even though they weren't making a lot of yards — 2.9 per carry, to be exact. In past playoff games, I can recall them forgetting that Edgerrin James was on the roster and getting panicky. But offensively, they showed the kind of patience they've shown all year. And was Dominic Rhodes any good? Both playoff games, he's come off the bench and given the Colts incredible energy.

C- **PASS OFFENSE:** OK, am I the only one who's just a teensy bit concerned about the way Peyton Manning has played in these playoffs? It's understood, the Ravens defense is crazy good. But I'm still looking for evidence that Manning can raise his game in the playoffs, or at least play as well in high-stakes games as he does all regular season. Watching Saturday's game, I kept wondering when Peyton turned into Trent Dilfer. You know, manage the game, limit mistakes and let the defense win it. (P.S.: That hurry-up stuff didn't work. Ditch it. Thank you.)

A **RUN DEFENSE:** Wow. How's that for journalistic insight? But what else can you say? Wow. It's incredible to me that this same group, minus a player or two, gave up 375 rushing yards to Jacksonville. All of a sudden, the Colts' defenders are playing the Dungy defense the way Tony's old Bucs used to play it. All year, they've been saying they were in the right position to make plays but just weren't making those plays. Personally, I think the change has something to do with cattle prods and other instruments of torture, but I can't be completely sure.

A **PASS DEFENSE:** One week ago, the Chiefs didn't get their initial first down until late in the third quarter. This week, the Ravens didn't have their first third-down conversion until late in the third quarter. Two sacks. Two interceptions — and it could have been more. I don't know if Nick Harper is having Ben Roethlisberger nightmares, but he has played this postseason like a man on a mission. He's not alone. If I'm Bob Sanders, honestly, I don't even bother playing next regular season. Just save it all for the playoffs.

A- **SPECIAL TEAMS:** A game like this, a defensive struggle where yards are hard to find, those hidden yards on special teams are huge. And so, by the way, are those five field goals by Adam Vinatieri, whose 51-yarder looked like Tiger's Masters chip in 2005, hanging on the edge before falling through. The Colts also got huge games from the kick-coverage team — where have they been all year? — and from return man Terrence Wilkins.

A **COACHING:** Late in Saturday's game, Tony Dungy shared a moment with Booger McFarland, who also played for Dungy in Tampa Bay. This, he said, was like the old days in Tampa, when every game seemed like it ended 9-6. Give Dungy and his coaching staff credit. They've kept this group believing, even after a brutal defensive regular season. They stuck to their guns, but also were willing to move out Gilbert Gardner and move in Rob Morris. Good challenge, too, on Todd Heap's early fumble, which set up the Colts' second field goal.

A+ **INTANGIBLES:** If you were brave enough to come to this game — and wore a Colts jersey and lived to tell about it — you know how nasty it was in and around the stadium Saturday. For the locals, this wasn't just a football game; it was a catharsis. They wanted to avenge what happened 23 years ago. It was as charged an atmosphere as I've ever experienced at a game. And the Colts were thoroughly unfazed.

SUPER AT LAST

MANNING'S DRIVE, DUNGY'S MILESTONE . . . AND A SUPER BOWL

By Mike Chappell

"I don't get into monkeys and vindication. I know how hard I've worked this year. I know how hard I've worked this week."

— Peyton Manning on whether Sunday's victory got the proverbial monkey off his back

The quarterback and team with so much on the line came up big in a beat-the-clock, beat-down-your-reputation moment Sunday evening inside a vibrating RCA Dome.

Peyton Manning, unable to deliver so many times in previous playoffs, delivered the Colts to their first Super Bowl of their Indy era, the first in more than three decades. He countered a spotty first half that saw the Colts

AFC Championship

Colts 38
Patriots 34

Team record: 15-4

◄**LET IT RAIN:** Colts cornerback Marlin Jackson bathes in the celebration after the Colts surged back from a 21-3 deficit. His interception of a Tom Brady pass with 16 seconds left sealed the win. **Matt Detrich** / The Star

▶**HOW SWEET IT IS!** Peyton Manning gets a well-deserved hug from his wife, Ashley, after the monumental win. **Sam Riche** / The Star

trail 21-3 with a sparkling second half, leading the Colts to a 38-34 victory over New England in the AFC Championship Game.

It was the largest comeback in conference championship history, AFC or NFC. And it was a long time coming for Manning, who had been 5-6 in previous postseason starts and 0-1 in conference-title-game appearances.

With the Dome pulsating and the game and his place in history on the line, Manning stepped behind center Jeff Saturday with 2 minutes, 17 seconds re-maining. First-and-10 at the Colts 20. One timeout. Trailing the Patriots 34-31.

A long way to go. A lot of ghosts to exorcise.

"There was no doubt in anybody's mind that we were going to take that ball down and score," coach Tony Dungy said.

No doubt that Manning would finally complete a dramatic drive in a humongous game? He entered the game with 28 game-winning drives in the fourth quarter or overtime. That included zero in the playoffs.

Seven plays and 80 yards later,

▲ **ROASTED BRADY:** Matt McDermand, Indianapolis, helps stuff a toy football into a roasting pig with a Tom Brady jersey. He and other fans tailgate at the corner of South and West Streets near the RCA Dome. **Robert Scheer** / The Star

◄ **TAKE A SWING:** Colts fan Scott Sanders, Indianapolis, slams a car painted with Patriots colors with a sledge hammer. Fans paid $5 for three hits on the car and the money was being donated to the St. Elizabeth House for battered women. **Matt Detrich** / The Star

Manning and the Colts had seized the moment. Rookie running back Joseph Addai slithered through the heart of the Patriots' defense, virtually untouched, for a 3-yard touchdown.

Colts 38, Patriots 34. Next stop, Feb. 4 in Miami, site of Super Bowl XLI.

Did Manning feel like he had finally yanked a 500-pound gorilla off his back?

"I just don't get into that. I don't play that card," Manning said. "I don't get into monkeys and vindication. I know how hard I've worked this year. I know how hard I've worked this week."

That work paid major dividends with everything on the line.

◀**PREGAME ADRENALINE:** Colts wide receiver Reggie Wayne gets revved up before the start of the the game.
Matt Detrich / The Star

◀**TOAST:** Indianapolis Mayor Bart Peterson cheers on the Colts with fans from the Blue Crew.
Matt Detrich / The Star

◀◀**FANATICS:** Colts fans Judy Mandzik (left) and Pete Volkleeck (center) both from Indy, cheer on the Colts as they leave the field after pregame warmups.
Sam Riche / The Star

Manning was 3-for-4 for 57 yards on the defining drive. He hit Reggie Wayne for 11 yards, Bryan Fletcher for 32 on second-and-10 and added another 14-yarder to Wayne. The last completion turned into a 26-yard gain when linebacker Tully Banta-Cain was penalized for making contact with Manning's helmet on his rush.

Presented with a first-and-10 at the 11, the Colts allowed Addai to do the rest.

"Those are dreams you always have as a kid," said Manning, who had to shake off a sore right thumb after he hit it on the helmet of tackle Tarik Glenn on the previous drive. "It's always nice when you can go out there and do it."

The dramatic ending was required because of an inefficient start. At the half, the Colts trailed 21-6 and Manning had completed just 13-of-24 passes for 124 yards and one interception.

▶ **SOLID COVERAGE:** Patriot cornerback Asante Samuel (right) breaks up a pass intended for Marvin Harrison in the first quarter. Sam Riche / The Star

▼ **GOING FOR MORE:** Dallas Clark gains some extra yards as he is brought down by Artrell Hawkins of the Patriots during first-quarter action. Robert Scheer / The Star

The interception was a costly one: cornerback Asante Samuel jumped Marvin Harrison's hook route and returned it 39 yards for a touchdown.

That made it 21-3.

"You certainly don't envision getting down 21-3 to the New England Patriots in any game, much less the playoffs," Manning said.

But after falling hard, the offense found its rhythm. It scored on six of its next eight possessions — four touchdowns and two Adam Vinatieri field goals.

For the game, Manning completed 27-of-47 passes for 349 yards and a 1-yard touchdown to defensive tackle/fullback Dan Klecko.

In the wild, confetti-strewn scene on the field afterward, Colts owner Jim Irsay accepted the Lamar Hunt Trophy, and made it clear there's still work to be done.

"It's an incredible day for us," he said. "I just couldn't be happier for our team and for all our fans.

"We have one more mission! One more mission in Miami! We're not done yet!" ■

◀**DENIED AGAIN:** Patriots cornerback Ellis Hobbs (27) tips the ball out of the reach of Colts wide receiver Reggie Wayne in the final seconds of the second quarter. **Matt Detrich** / The Star

◀◀**BIG HIT:** Colts defensive back Bob Sanders (21) puts a hard hit on Patriots running back Heath Evans in the second quarter.
Matt Detrich / The Star

◀**QUICK BREAK TO THE BALL:** Patriots cornerback Asante Samuel (22) picks off a Peyton Manning pass in front of Colts wide receiver Marvin Harrison in the second quarter. Samuel returned the interception for a touchdown.
Robert Scheer / The Star

KRAVITZ ON THE COLTS

2.17 minutes of magic.

The gremlins, the ghosts, the whispers, the doubts, all of them, gone in that one 2-minute and 17-second snapshot of excellence. We will never look at the Indianapolis Colts quite the same way again. And certainly, clearly, we will never look at Manning as the best never to do this or do that, because he's done it, did it after a brutish first half, did it after his interception sent the Colts behind by a 21-3 score, did it facing unimaginable pressure.

It's said anything truly worthwhile comes with a struggle, with heartache and disappointment, and the Colts have known plenty of that the past few Januarys. But there is a gritty nobility to this team, coming back and coming back, putting up those four straight seasons of 12-or-more victories despite the harsh way each prior season had ended.

Let this one sink in: The Indianapolis Colts, producers of the greatest comeback ever in a conference championship game, are going to the Super Bowl.

▲ **MOMENTUM SHIFT:** Colts wide receiver Marvin Harrison pulls in a pass over New England cornerback Asante Samuel in the third quarter.
Matt Detrich / The Star

▶ **TURNING UP THE HEAT:** Colts defensive end Dwight Freeney (93) puts pressure on Patriots quarterback Tom Brady in the third quarter.
Matt Kryger / The Star

▶▶ **THE BIG MAN SCORES:** Colts center Jeff Saturday spikes the ball after he recovered a fumble by running back Dominic Rhodes for a touchdown to tie the score in the fourth quarter.
Matt Detrich / The Star

▲ **UNTOUCHED:** Joseph Addai scores the game-winner. **Robert Scheer** / The Star

◀ **FAN SUPPORT:** Colts defensive tackle Darrell Reid is cheered by fans after he stopped a New England kickoff return dead in their tracks in the third quarter. **Matt Detrich** / The Star

◀ **PERFORMING UNDER PRESSURE:** Manning gets his pass off under pressure from the Pats' Ty Warren in the fourth quarter. **Sam Riche** / The Star

▶ **SEALING THE DEAL:** Colts players Antoine Bethea (41) and Kelvin Hayden (26) celebrate the interception by Colts defensive back Marlin Jackson (28) as Robert Mathis (98) hugs him. **Sam Riche** / The Star

Dancing their way to Miami

Colts celebrate after finally getting past Patriots in playoffs

By Phil Richards

There was dancing on the midfield horseshoe helmet at the RCA Dome on Sunday night, but this wasn't another over-the-top New England celebration.

Safety Marlin Jackson intercepted a Tom Brady pass with 16 seconds to play to clinch the Indianapolis Colts' 38-34 victory in the AFC Championship Game. Jackson did the dancing, accompanied almost unanimously by the roaring sellout crowd of 57,433.

Twenty-three years after the Mayflower moving vans delivered the Baltimore Colts to Indianapolis, the Colts have delivered a Super Bowl to a championship-starved city. Indianapolis hasn't celebrated a major professional title since the Indiana Pacers won an ABA banner in 1973.

The Colts will meet the Chicago Bears in Super Bowl XLI on Feb. 4 in Dolphin Stadium in Miami. It will be a show-down between old friends and the first two black head coaches to take teams to the Super Bowl.

Lovie Smith, whose Bears beat New Orleans 39-14 earlier Sunday, served as an assistant coach under Dungy from 1996 through 2000 at Tampa Bay.

▲ **VICTORY HUG:** Reggie Wayne (right) hugs Marvin Harrison after defeating the Patriots in the AFC Championship Game.
Matt Kryger / The Star

That can wait. The Colts and their leather-lunged crowd had reason to party Sunday. They slew the dragon, vanquished the ghosts, exorcised the demons of playoffs past. The proud Patriots have won the Super Bowl three of the past five years. They twice dismissed the Colts along the way: in the 2003 AFC Championship Game and in a 2004 divisional game.

Sunday's game was one charged with emotion, big hits and big plays, and the Colts came through with a champion's heart. They came back from a 21-3 deficit, the largest comeback in conference championship history.

"Not the hole you want to be in," quarterback Peyton

◀**PACK YOUR BAGS:** Colts fans celebrate the win. **Sam Riche** / The Star

Manning said.

Comebacks are supposed to be Brady's specialty. He brought the Patriots from a fourth-quarter deficit or tie six times while winning 12 of his first 13 playoff games as a starter.

Sunday night was Manning's turn. Playing under the enormous pressure of past playoff failures, the Colts quarterback completed 27-of-47 passes for 349 yards and one touchdown and ran for another as he engineered his first postseason fourth-quarter comeback victory.

"I'm really happy for Peyton," Dungy said. "He was very, very calm. He had to bring us from behind three or four times. It was fitting.

"Peyton Manning's a great player, and anybody who

▲**SOMETHING TO CHEER ABOUT:** Colts cheerleaders rejoice near the end of the game. **Robert Scheer** / The Star

◀**BIG CELEBRATION:** The Colts' Dwight Freeney celebrates the victory. **Matt Kryger** / The Star

doesn't know that doesn't know much about football."

The game-winner was running back Joseph Addai's 3-yard touchdown run with exactly one minute to play.

Tight end Dallas Clark caught six passes for 137 yards as the Colts overcame a couple of breakdowns in kickoff and punt coverage, two fourth downs on which they yielded 62 yards and a defense that struggled much of the night.

"We talked a lot at halftime about how we just had to keep our poise and continue to play to have a chance in the fourth quarter," Dungy said.

That final chance came with the Colts trailing 34-31. They had the football on their own 20. Eighty yards to cover and 2:17 and a single timeout with which to do it.

◀ **WE DID IT:** Colts coach Tony Dungy reacts with the fans after the win. Sam Riche / The Star

▼ **POSTGAME PASSING:** Patriots coach Bill Belichick (left) heads off the field after congratulating Peyton Manning. Robert Scheer / The Star

Manning completed 3-of-4 passes to take the Colts to the New England 11. The big plays were a 32-yard pass to tight end Bryan Fletcher and a roughing-the-passer penalty on Patriots linebacker Tully Banta-Cain.

Three times Manning handed off to Addai, who finally blasted untouched through a hole on the right side behind guard Jake Scott and tackle Ryan Diem for the decisive touchdown. Addai continued through the end zone and leaped to the top of the stadium wall, where he was embraced by fans.

The Colts scored on six of their final eight possessions, not counting a kneel-down, and twice did it in unorthodox fashion.

Defensive tackle Dan Klecko, a sometimes fullback, caught a 1-yard touchdown pass. Center Jeff Saturday fell on a Dominic Rhodes fumble for another touchdown.

So the Colts wide bodies outscored New England's 14-7. Patriots guard Logan Mankins recovered a botched handoff in the end zone for a New England touchdown.

After New England cornerback Asante Samuel's 39-yard interception return for a touchdown made it 21-3, the Colts answered with drives of 80, 76, 76, 67, 59 and 80 yards. They just kept coming.

"Obviously, there's a lot of emotion in the locker room," Dungy said. "I've never been prouder. We had to do it the hard way. We had to go through a champion and we were down 18 points to them."

Brady finished with 21 completions in 34 pass attempts for 232 yards and one touchdown. ∎

THE INDIANAPOLIS STAR

A GANNETT NEWSPAPER
• INDYSTAR.COM •

"Where the Spirit of the Lord Is, there is Liberty" II Cor. 3:17

— MONDAY, JANUARY 22, 2007 —

CITY FINAL
★ 50 CENTS

38 🏈 34

★★ AFC CHAMPIONSHIP EDITION ★★

BLUE HEAVEN!

COLTS SEIZE FIRST INDY-ERA SUPER BOWL BID

LET IT RAIN: Indianapolis Colts cornerback Martin Jackson bathes in the celebration after the Colts surged back from a 21-3 deficit. His interception of a Tom Brady pass with 16 seconds left in the game sealed the win.

MATT DETRICH / The Star

Manning, Colts break through with 2:17 of magic

BOB KRAVITZ

See Kravitz, Page A9

SUPER BOWL XLI
COLTS VS. BEARS
Sunday, February 4 ◆ Miami, Fla.

COMPLETE COVERAGE INSIDE
16-page Colts victory section
Get more insight into the Colts' thrilling comeback win over the New England Patriots.

◉ **INDYSTAR.COM/COLTS**
Photos, video and more
Photo galleries: See the best images of the game and playoff-hungry Colts fans.
Video: Watch jubilant Colts fans leaving the RCA Dome.
Audio slideshow: Experience a supercharged night at the Dome.

GET YOUR SOUVENIRS
Front-page reprints, T-shirts available
Readers can purchase them online at IndyStar.com or at The Star. Details, A9

The Patriots curse ends; countdown to Miami begins

WEATHER		INDEX
Low 28 High 32	Cloudy, with flurries possible. Full forecast, B6	

INDIANA LIFE SCIENCES INITIATIVE
lifesciences.iu.edu

IU INDIANA UNIVERSITY
Turning Breakthroughs into Business

STATE LAWMAKERS WADE IN 1,420 BILLS Mountain of legislation covers public safety, social issues, taxes and ideas that are just a bit out there. B1

▶ **FUTURE RECEIVER?:** Colts wide receiver Marvin Harrison smiles as he holds his son, Marvin, after the Colts defeated the New England Patriots 38-34. **Matt Kryger** / The Star

▼ **HAPPY OWNER:** Colts owner Jim Irsay (right) and team president Bill Polian laugh after the game. **Robert Scheer** / The Star

▶ **EMOTIONAL MOMENT:** Colts offensive coordinator Tom Moore takes in a moment by himself on the bench after the win. **Matt Detrich** / The Star

▶▶ **THANKS, FANS:** Dallas Clark celebrates.
Sam Riche / The Star

▶PARTY ON THE CIRCLE: Sarah Craft, Indianapolis, rejoices at Monument Circle following the Colts' win. **Rob Goebel** / The Star

▼PARTY IN THE DOME: Colts linebacker Cato June screams in celebration in the confetti as he is lifted onto the shoulders of Terry Dixon (center) and Terrance Jackson (right). **Matt Detrich** / The Star

⬆ CAN'T STOP SMILING: Colts coach Tony Dungy smiles as he answers questions from the media during a news conference the morning after the game. **Matt Kryger** / The Star

▲ FAMIILY GATHERING: Peyton Manning (center) talks with his brothers Cooper (left) and Eli after the awards presentation at the center of the field. **Robert Scheer** / The Star

◀TROPHY CELEBRATION: Colts coach Tony Dungy holds up the AFC trophy as he celebrates with team president Bill Polian and the players at the RCA Dome. **Mike Fender** / The Star

Indy's long road to the Super Bowl

By George McLaren

The road to the Super Bowl for the Indianapolis Colts began 23 years ago in an empty stadium.

In the early 1980s, Indianapolis city officials, led by then-Mayor William Hudnut, spent $77.5 million to build a state-of-the-art football stadium with an inflatable roof called the Hoosier Dome.

There was a catch, and it was a doozy: Indy had no NFL team to put in it.

But in classic "if you build it, they will come" style, the city suddenly produced a team to go with its stadium when Mayflower moving vans arrived after leaving Baltimore in the dead of night in 1984.

It wasn't the first time that a Colts football team had switched cities.

According to the Colts' official team history, the lineage goes back to Sept. 7, 1947, when a pro football team calling itself the Colts played its first game in Baltimore after relocating from Miami. It soon disbanded because of financial difficulties.

A second Colts team arose in 1953 — also a transplant, this time from Dallas. Under the leadership of quarterback Johnny Unitas, the Baltimore Colts won back-to-back NFL championships in 1958 and 1959 before the Super Bowl was created. In January 1969, the Colts lost Super Bowl III to Joe Namath and the New York Jets. They followed that up with a Super Bowl victory in 1971 over the Dallas Cowboys.

The next year, businessman Robert Irsay acquired the Colts from then owner Carroll Rosenbloom in exchange for the Los Angeles Rams.

The Baltimore club had its ups and downs over the next decade, with three consecutive AFC Eastern Division titles beginning in 1975, followed by six consecutive losing seasons — including a winless year in 1982 during a strike-shortened schedule. Fans were angry, attendance was down and rumors began circulating that Irsay would move the team elsewhere.

Meanwhile, Indianapolis began courting Irsay in secret negotiations. It was a good match. Indianapolis was desperate to fill its stadium, while Irsay feared the Maryland state legislature was about to take his away from him.

After Irsay said yes, Hudnut placed a call to a friend who owned a moving company. Mayflower trucks rolled up late on March 28, 1984. After mid-

▲ **WARM WELCOME:** Indianapolis Mayor William Hudnut welcomes Mayflower moving vans filled with Indianapolis Colts possessions in March 1984. **File photo** / The Star

▲ **FAMILY BUSINESS:** Robert Irsay (right) owned the Colts from 1970 until his death in 1997 when control of the team passed to his son Jim (left). **File photo** / The Star

night, in a snowstorm, the trucks headed in different directions to disguise their destination.

When the news broke, Baltimore fans were enraged, but Irsay and the team received heroes' welcomes in Indianapolis. Fans placed 143,000 requests for season tickets in a 60,000-seat stadium.

The honeymoon feeling began to fade as the new Indianapolis Colts struggled through mediocre seasons and what seemed at times to be a revolving door of head coaches, and some questionable player decisions.

The Colts had already lost out on future Hall of Famer John Elway but then squandered two top players plus draft picks to obtain local football hero — but major disappointment — Jeff George. He was later traded.

But premier running backs Eric Dickerson and Marshall Faulk, as well as popular quarterback Jim "Captain Comeback" Harbaugh, still gave fans something to cheer about and modest success in those early years kept many fans hopeful. The Colts made the playoffs a few times in that

era, most notably in 1995 when Harbaugh was one pass away from the Super Bowl. In a moment replayed over and over, his "Hail Mary" to receiver Aaron Bailey bounced to the turf in the end zone at Pittsburgh, ending a what-might-have-been season.

In 1997, after the death of Robert Irsay, son Jim took over ownership of the team. The following year the Colts had a first-round draft pick and used it to acquire Tennessee quarterback Peyton Manning.

In Manning's rookie season the Colts recorded their second consecutive 3-13 season. But in 1999, team fortunes turned with the selection of another promising rookie, running back Edgerrin James. "The Triplets" — James, Manning and receiver Marvin Harrison — turned the Colts into a 13-3 powerhouse, fueling the biggest one-season record turnaround in NFL history.

The Colts made the playoffs again in 2000 and 2002, but lost both times in the first round. In 2003, they finished 12-4, won the AFC South and reached the AFC Championship Game. And in the 2004 season, Manning broke Dan Marino's single-season touchdown record. But both years the Colts' postseason ended in the snow at Foxborough, Mass., with heartbreaking losses to Tom Brady's New England Patriots.

The 2005 season seem destined to be The Year. For the first five games the Colts

▲ **BAD TIMES:** Fans hide their heads under grocery bags during this 31-17 loss to the Jets on Nov. 15, 1993. The Colts posted a 4-12 season record that year, their 10th season in Indianapolis. **Mike Fender** / The Star

▲ **TOP PICK:** Peyton Manning, the NFL's No. 1 draft pick in 1998, holds up his new Colts jersey on April 18, 1998, as his parents, Archie and Olivia, look on. Colts coach Jim Mora is at right. **Matt Kryger** / The Star

defense held opponents to 10 points or less while Manning and his receivers were unstoppable. In Week 7, Manning and Harrison connected for their 86th career touchdown — an NFL record. And then the Colts hammered the Patriots 40-21 at Gillette Stadium. It was Manning's first win after seven stumbles at New England, and snapped a nine-game Colts road losing streak in the series dating to 1996.

The Colts kept winning and the buzz was an undefeated season and a sure trip to the Super Bowl. The streak ended at 13 games and the Colts finished with an NFL-best 14-2 record, a first-round playoff bye and homefield advantage. But that seemingly magic year ended abruptly in a 21-18 playoff loss to the Pittsburgh Steelers.

Fans were stunned and many grumbled that Manning just couldn't win the big ones. Then the 2006 season began and hope returned — maybe *this* would be the year.

BLUE REIGN

BELIEVE IT INDIANAPOLIS: COLTS ARE WORLD CHAMPS

By Phil Richards

MIAMI — No more suggestions of "soft." No more snide "dome" team references. No more finesse label. No more playoff questions.

The Indianapolis Colts smashed every stereotype Sunday evening while they were smashing the big, bad, bruising Chicago Bears 29-17 to win Super Bowl XLI at rainy, soggy Dolphin Stadium.

The Colts pounded the Bears with their running game. They battered them with a swarming, attacking defense. They punished. The Colts' fat 430-265 advantage in total yards was more indicative of their dominance than was the scoreboard.

The Colts ran 81 plays to Chicago's 48 and outrushed them 191 yards — a Colts' postseason record — to 111.

"Now it's time to party. Now we can just let loose and enjoy it," said safety Bob Sanders, who intercepted one pass, broke up another and

Super Bowl

Colts 29
Bears 17

Team record: 16-4

◀ **VICTORY KISS:** Colts safety Bob Sanders kisses the Vince Lombardi Trophy following the Colts' 29-17 victory in Super Bowl XLI. Matt Kryger / The Star

▶ **AT LAST:** Colts quarterback and Super Bowl MVP Peyton Manning hoists the Vince Lombardi Trophy in the air after the Colts defeated the Chicago Bears. Matt Detrich / The Star

forced a fumble.

Peyton Manning, long derided as a quarterback who put up big numbers but didn't win big games, won the biggest one Sunday. Manning completed 25-of-38 passes for 247 yards and one touchdown with one interception.

With the dank postgame air still full of smoke, streamers, confetti and fireworks, the announcement was made: Manning had won the Pete Rozelle Trophy as the game's Most Valuable Player. He got

▶ **LIGHT SHOW:** Dolphin Stadium in South Florida is awash in blue lights the night before the Indianapolis Colts take on the Chicago Bears in the Super Bowl. The lights would alternate between Colts and Bears colors.
Mike Fender / The Star

▶ **BLUE SUNDAY:** Father Phil Bowers took to the lectern sporting a Colts blue vestment at the end of the service Sunday at Holy Spirit Parish in Fishers. He received a standing ovation from the congregation.
Scott Goldman / The Star

▶▶ **FILING IN FOR THE GAME:** Bears and Colts fans alike stream through the gates at 3:45 p.m. for Super Bowl XLI, which didn't kick off until 6:25 p.m. **Sam Riche** / The Star

his ring and more.

He deferred to the team.

"That's been our theme all year; we have won as a team," Manning said. "Everybody did their part. There was no panic, nobody gave up. We stayed calm the entire game. We truly won this championship as a team and I'm proud to be part of it."

The world title was the Colts' fourth in 54 years as NFL members, but their first in 23 seasons in Indianapolis, their first since the Baltimore Colts won Super Bowl V after the 1970 season.

The Colts celebrated by dumping not one but two buckets of Gatorade on their coach, Tony Dungy.

"This may not be one of our most talented teams but it sure was the one that felt the most love for one another, the most connection," said Dungy, the first black coach to win the Super Bowl. "I love these guys. I know what they went through to win this."

Dungy became only the third man to win a Super Bowl

▼ **THE KICKOFF:** Super Bowl fans catch the opening kick-off on their cameras (flashes in the stadium) as the Colts' Adam Vinatieri kicks the ball.
Sam Riche / The Star

ring as a player and a coach. He was a backup safety and special teams player with Pittsburgh when the Steelers won Super Bowl XIII after the 1978 season. Mike Ditka and Tom Flores also have accomplished the double.

The Bears had scored 66 points in two playoff games while allowing only 38. They hadn't met a team like the Colts, whose defense and running game were rejuvenated during their four-game playoff run. Bears fans dominated the crowd of 74,512. On the field, it was another story.

Running backs Dominic Rhodes and Joseph Addai were the 1-2 punch that knocked out the Bears' fifth-ranked defense. Rhodes rushed 21 times for 113 yards and a touchdown. Addai ran 19 times for 77 yards and caught 10 passes for 66 yards. The rookie's reception total

was one shy of the Super Bowl record shared by Pro Football Hall of Famer Jerry Rice and two others.

With the offensive line asserting its will, the Colts had the prescription for success: The team that has

▶ **THAT DIDN'T TAKE LONG:** Devin Hester of the Bears runs back the opening kickoff 92 yards for a touchdown. Hester, who returned six kicks (kickoffs, punts and a missed field goal) for touchdowns during the regular season, is the first player in Super Bowl history to return the opening kickoff for a touchdown. The Colts had trouble covering kickoffs all season. Matt Kryger / The Star

▶ **THIS IS TOO EASY:** Colts wide receiver Reggie Wayne runs into the end zone after catching a long pass from Peyton Manning in the first quarter. He finished with two catches for 61 yards. This reception went for 53 yards and brought the Colts back to within 7-6. Matt Kryger / The Star

rushed for more yards has won 34 of the 41 Super
Bowls.

"Dom gave us a great lift," Dungy said. "He and
Joseph did a great job going up against a great defense, but really, it was just our whole team fighting
and I'm very proud of them."

Chicago quarterback Rex Grossman had a forgettable night. He completed 20-of-28 passes for 165
yards and a touchdown. He also twice fumbled snaps
— losing 11 yards on one, possession on the other
— and threw a pair of interceptions, one of which was

◄**NOT SO FAST:** Colts running back Joseph Addai is pulled down by Bears
Ian Scott (left), Danieal Manning (38) and Brian Urlacher during the
second quarter. **Matt Detrich** / The Star

▼**HE'S GOING IN:** Dominic Rhodes barrels into the end zone for a second-
quarter touchdown. Rhodes rushed for 113 yards, including a long of 36
yards, and also had one reception for 8 yards. **Matt Kryger** / The Star

◀◀FUMBLE!: Colts defensive end Dwight Freeney (93) goes after a Bears fumble in the second quarter. **Matt Detrich** / The Star

◀CELEBRATION: Colts defensive end Robert Mathis celebrates the recovery of a Bears fumble in the second quarter. **Matt Detrich** / The Star

▼FITTING SONG CHOICE: Prince sings "Purple Rain" during the halftime show. **Robert Scheer** / The Star

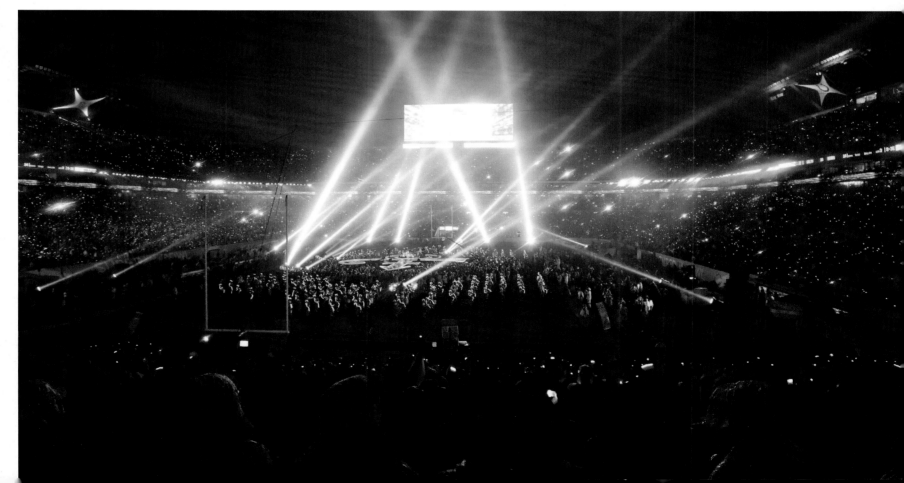

▲ **SACK CELEBRATION:** The Colts' Anthony McFarland (92) and Robert Mathis celebrate after a third- quarter sack of Chicago quarterback Rex Grossman. **Sam Riche** / The Star

▲ **GO COLTS!:** Back in Indianapolis, Kortney Price (left) and Janet Higgins, both from Indy cheer the Colts in the second half. Colts fans flocked to the Blue Crew Sports Grill to watch the game. **Rob Goebel** / The Star

▼ **TURNING UP THE HEAT:** Colts defensive tackle Raheem Brock puts a hit on Bears quarterback Rex Grossman, knocking his chinstrap up to his nose in the third quarter. **Matt Detrich** / The Star

returned 56 yards by backup cornerback Kelvin Hayden for the clinching touchdown.

It was a bizarre first half that featured steady rain, slippery footballs and six turnovers. Twice the teams traded fumbles on consecutive snaps.

◄THE BIG PLAY: Kelvin Hayden's fourth-quarter interception and 56-yard return for a touchdown off a wobbly pass by Bears quarterback Rex Grossman sealed the outcome of the Colts' Super Bowl victory. **Matt Kryger** / The Star

▼ HEADED FOR PAYDIRT: Colts defensive back Kelvin Hayden runs back his interception for a touchdown that put the Colts up 29-17. **Matt Detrich** / The Star

The game began with a bolt of lightning where there was no thunder. The Colts had the temerity to direct the opening kickoff to Pro Bowl return man Devin Hester. He returned it 92 yards for a touchdown.

That and a 52-yard run by Thomas Jones that set up the Bears' second touchdown were the only big plays made by Chicago.

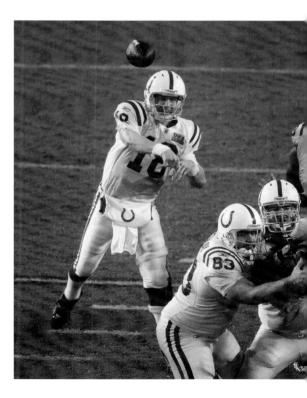

▲ FINDING HIS TARGET: Peyton Manning passes during third-quarter action. **Robert Scheer** / The Star

SECTION P | MONDAY, FEBRUARY 5, 2007 | THE INDIANAPOLIS STAR
INDYSTAR.COM/COLTS | 40-PAGE SPECIAL SECTION IN TWO PARTS

SUPER BOWL

COLTS 29, BEARS 17

BLUE REIGN

BELIEVE IT, INDIANAPOLIS: COLTS ARE WORLD CHAMPS

Colts safety Bob Sanders

COLTS LEAVE NO DOUBT
The Colts impose their will nearly all game, with Joseph Addai and Dominic Rhodes pounding the ball on the ground and their resurgent defense stuffing the run and bringing out the "Bad Rex" in QB Rex Grossman. **P2**

MANNING REACHES MOUNTAINTOP
Quarterback Peyton Manning silences any remaining critics in MVP fashion, winning the Pete Rozelle award as the Super Bowl's most outstanding player for his 247-yard, one-touchdown performance. **P4**

A SUPER NIGHT ON TV
Prince rocks the house with a stirring halftime show that includes a fiery rendition of "Let's Go Crazy." Commercials starring Jay-Z, Dale Earnhardt Jr. and David Letterman and Oprah also are part of a flawless night on TV. **P6**

WHOOPING IT UP IN THE RAIN
Indianapolis fans show up in force at the Super Bowl to cheer their team to an NFL championship. The Star takes a look in photos and words at their rainy and rowdy visit to Miami. **P30-31**

▶ **BRINGING THE PRESSURE:** Colts defensive end Robert Mathis (98) soars toward Bears quarterback Rex Grossman (8) in the fourth quarter. Sam Riche / The Star

The Colts had numerous opportunities but got little traction. They scored on a 53-yard Manning pass to wide receiver Reggie Wayne on which Chicago blew coverage. A mishandled snap cost them the point-after attempt but the AFC champions moved ahead on the first of Adam Vinatieri's three field goals and Rhodes' 1-yard touchdown run.

The victory validated the Colts' era of excellence. Since the start of the 1999 season, their 89-39 regular-season record is the league's best. They are the only team that has made the playoffs seven times over those eight years. The Colts and the Dallas Cowboys (1992-95) are the only teams in NFL history to win 12 or more games in four successive seasons.

No longer will those achievements be dismissed because of the Colts' playoff failures. No longer will they be referred to as a dome team, as a finesse team. They are champions, for life. ∎

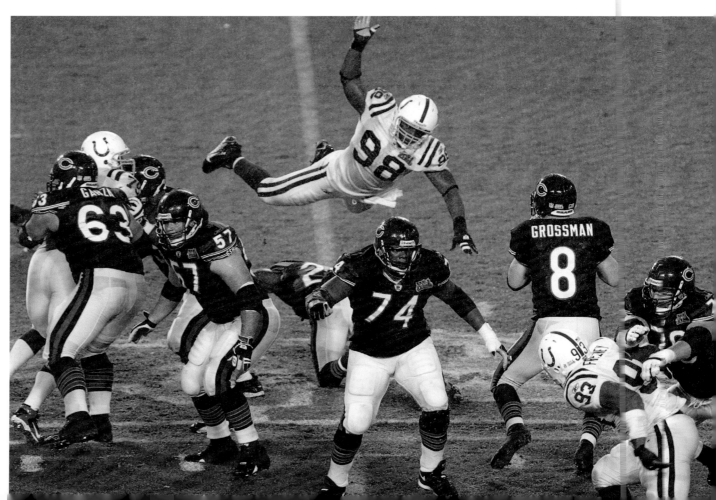

▲ **I'LL TAKE THAT:** Colts safety Bob Sanders (21) intercepts a pass intended for the Bears' Bernard Berrian (80) in the fourth quarter. **Sam Riche** / The Star

▲ **DOUBLE-BARREL BATH:** Coach Tony Dungy gets a Gatorade bath after the win. **Sam Riche** / The Star

▼ **VICTORY RIDE:** Colts coach Tony Dungy gets a ride on the shoulders of assistant coaches and players after his team won the Super Bowl. **Sam Riche** / The Star

Lone mark against Manning erased

Even before Super Bowl title, Colts quarterback was Hall of Fame player, Dungy says

By Mike Chappell

MIAMI — The rain that soaked a sellout crowd at Dolphin Stadium on Sunday night washed away the stigma, once and for all, that had attached itself to Peyton Manning so long ago.

He didn't just win a big game. He won the biggest game the NFL has to offer.

But after being voted the Most Valuable Player of Super Bowl XLI by passing for 247 yards and one touchdown in the Indianapolis Colts' 29-17 win over the Chicago Bears, Manning declined to thumb his nose at his detractors.

"I've never played that card," he said.

Tony Dungy didn't hesitate to play it. His eyes glistened when asked if Manning winning a Super Bowl in his ninth season would end the criticism that the two-time NFL MVP was missing something — a championship gene, something — that had kept him from taking a team to a national title at the University of Tennessee or an NFL title with the Colts.

"You know, I don't know," Dungy said. "Maybe people now will say, 'If he doesn't win two in a row, it's not

▲ **CHAMPS AT LAST:** It was a first for Tony Dungy (left), who tasted Super Bowl success in his 11th season leading an NFL team. It was also a first for Peyton Manning, who at last answered questions about his ability to win the big one. **Matt Kryger** / The Star

good enough.'

"Peyton Manning is a tremendous player who's a great leader. He prepares, he works, he does everything that you can do to win ball games and to lead your team."

Dungy was just getting warmed up. It was clear he took great exception to previous criticism of a quarterback who entered the game with numerous regular-season records — 49 touchdown passes and a 121.1 rating in 2004 among them — but was just 6-6 in the postseason and had zero Super Bowl appearances.

Manning, his coach insisted, was great long before a wet and wild Sunday night in South Florida.

"If people think you had to win a Super Bowl to know that and validate it and justify it, that's just wrong," Dungy said. "But he's done it. He's got that behind him. I don't think there's anything you can say now other than this guy is a Hall of Fame player, one of the greatest players to ever play the game."

So there.

Manning didn't provide lightning bolts to accentuate the game-long rain. The damp field and damp ball wouldn't allow it.

What he did, after suffering an interception that ended the Colts' first possession, was take care of the football, distribute the football, manage the game. Seven players caught at least one pass; rookie running back Joseph Addai had a ca-

▲ **MUTUAL RESPECT:** Colts coach Tony Dungy hands the Vince Lombardi Trophy to quarterback Peyton Manning following the Colts' 29-17 win in Super Bowl XLI. Matt Kryger / The Star

◄ **RETURN ON INVESTMENT:** Colts owner Jim Irsey lifts the Vince Lombardi Trophy with coach Tony Dungy following the Colts' victory. Sam Riche / The Star

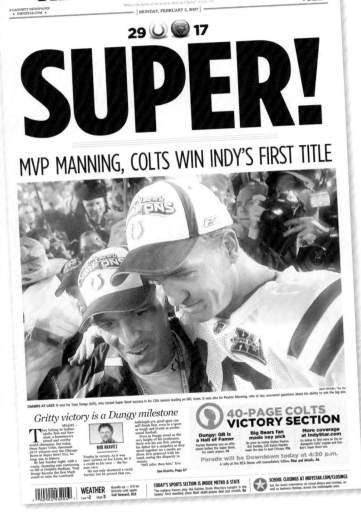

▶**HISTORY-MAKING PAIR:** Bears coach Lovie Smith (left) and Colts coach Tony Dungy greet each other following the Colts' 29-17 win in Super Bowl XLI. **Matt Kryger** / The Star

reer-best 10 for 66 yards. Reggie Wayne had just two catches, but one was a 53-yard touchdown when the Bears' safeties apparently botched their coverage and allowed Wayne to blow past them for an easy catch-and-run.

The running game was crisp and powerful. It pounded the Bears' No. 6-ranked run defense for a club postseason-record 191 yards on 42 carries. Dominic Rhodes had 113 yards on 21 carries while Addai added 77 yards on 19 attempts.

Manning was in control. That included his demeanor after the game.

A reporter mentioned that he seemed to be remarkably calm considering the circumstances.

"It's hit me," Manning said. "It was an emotional game and I think everybody is really drained right now. We put a lot of hard work and effort into this.

"I'll enjoy it tonight. We'll have a good time together. I'll celebrate with my teammates, and my family is here."

So cool, so composed just minutes after hoisting the sterling silver Vince Lombardi Trophy into the air.

"It's all happening pretty fast right now," Manning said. "This is kind of how I am, I guess. I'm excited. I'm

▼ **FAN CELEBRATION:** Colts fans outside Jillian's, at Georgia and Meridian streets, spontaneously jump onto the truck of Herb Moore as he drove his family through Downtown following the Colts' victory over the Chicago Bears. Waving the flag on top of the truck is Dustin Hackleman, Cicero, Ind.
Charlie Nye / The Star

proud to be on this team. I think this is something we'll enjoy for quite some time.

"I wanted to be on a team that won the Super Bowl. To me, that's what it's always been about. In years past when our team has come up short, it's been disappointing. But somehow, some way we have found a way to learn from some of those losses.

"We're a better team because of it." ■

▶**PANDEMONIUM:** Jay Bowling (arm raised) is in the middle of celebrating Colt fans when the game ends with an Indy win. Colts fans flocked to the Blue Crew Sports Grill to watch the Colts and Bears in the Super Bowl. **Rob Goebel** / The Star

▶▶**JUBILATION** Jubilant fans celebrate on Monument Circle after the Indianapolis Colts beat the Chicago Bears in Super Bowl XLI. **Charlie Nye** / The Star

▼**CHAMPS!:** Ryan Cole, Cincinnati, waves a newspaper with a headline that says "Champs!" The IPL Building illuminates the street with the Colts' signature horseshoe at Monument Circle in Downtown Indianapolis. **Heather Charles**/ The Star

▲ **CHAMPION'S WELCOME:** Colts coach Tony Dungy holds up the Vince Lombardi Trophy as the team enters the RCA Dome for a rally the day after the Super Bowl victory. Colts president Bill Polian stands behind him.

Joe Vitti / The Star